DOGS AT

MILITARY CANINE HEROES

WAR

CONNIE GOLDSMITH

TFCB

TWENTY-FIRST CENTURY BOOKS / MINNEAPOLIS

Acknowledgments: The author especially wishes to thank John C. Burnam, dog handler in the Vietnam War and powerful advocate for military working dogs, for his ongoing support and assistance with this project. Thanks also go to the people who took the time to speak with me about their experience with military working dogs: Courtney Griffin, Charlie Hardesty, Lora Harrist, Dr. Stewart Hilliard, Angela Lowe, Dr. Emily Pieracci, Bret Reynolds, Karl Stefanowicz, and Dustin Weeks.

Twenty-First Century Books
A division of Lerner Publishing Group, Inc.
241 First Avenue North
Minneapolis, MN 55401 USA

For reading levels and more information, look up this title at www.lernerbooks.com.

Main body text set in Adriana Condensed 11/15
Typeface provided by Chank.

Library of Congress Cataloging-in-Publication Data

Names: Goldsmith, Connie, 1945– author.
Title: Dogs at war: military canine heroes / by Connie Goldsmith.
Description: Minneapolis : Twenty-First Century Books, [2017] | Includes bibliographical references and index.
Identifiers: LCCN 2016009413 (print) | LCCN 2016018684 (ebook) | ISBN 9781512410129 (lb : alk. paper) |
    ISBN 9781512428520 (eb pdf)
Subjects: LCSH: Dogs—War use—United States.
Classification: LCC UH100 .G653 2016 (print) | LCC UH100 (ebook) | DDC 355.4/24—dc23

LC record available at https://lccn.loc.gov/2016009413

Manufactured in the United States of America
1-39560-21259-6/10/2016

CONTENTS

CHAPTER 1
TWO DOGS—TWO WARS

Americans love their dogs. Nearly half the households in the United States own at least one dog, and many families own two or more. Dogs want to play ball with us or chase a Frisbee or chomp a special treat we give them. There's nothing like a warm dog curled up next to us on a rainy day or a cold nose pressed against our arm when we're feeling sad. All a dog asks for is to be close to its person. People who live with dogs know how deep and strong the human-dog bond goes.

One of the strongest human-dog bonds is between a military working dog (MWD) and its handler. Six legs. Four eyes. Two hearts. One team. The dog and handler live together, eat together, play together, often sleep together, and risk their lives for each other every day while in a war zone. Experts say each military dog saves between 150 to 200 soldiers during its working life. It does so by sniffing

"We have a bond with these dogs that are as attached to us as we are to them. I have gone to war with this dog, and I would do it again in a heartbeat. I will go to the end of the world and back again for this dog, and I know he would do the same."

—Joel Townsend, handler for military working dog A-Taq in the Iraq War

Staff Sergeant Stephanie Pecovsky and her military working dog take a break during a ruck march training. In this exercise, a dog learns to walk at a relatively fast pace over distance while carrying a load.

out concealed bombs and weapons and by alerting its handler to hidden enemy soldiers.

Meet Mike Dowling and Rex, and John Burnam and Clipper. These outstanding teams worked in two wars separated by time and space, with very different outcomes for the heroic dogs.

WAR DOG TEAM IN IRAQ: MIKE AND REX

"This is arguably the single most dangerous place in the most dangerous war in the world right now," Mike Dowling said, writing about the time when he and Rex climbed out of a helicopter at the US Marine base at Mahmoudiyah, Iraq, in 2004. "And Rex and I have come here to do the most dangerous job in the world—tracking down the [rebel's hidden stash of] arms and explosives, plus their murderous improvised explosive devices." In 2004 Mike had every reason to worry. Soldiers in the US-led Iraq War (2003–2011) called this camp the capital of Iraq's Triangle of Death, an area south of Baghdad known for horrific violence.

Mike was twenty-two years old when he joined the US Marines in 2001. He served in the marines until 2005 and in the US Army Reserve from 2008 to 2010. His partner Rex came to the United States as a puppy from one of the top German shepherd breeders in Europe. Rex went through the US military's dog training school at Lackland Air Force Base in San Antonio, Texas, where he learned to identify and locate explosives by scent. On graduation, Rex's report card said, "Rex is an independent dog who will search of his own accord if the handler allows it. He has excellent odor recognition and will track the odor until he pinpoints source."

Rex was eighteen months old when he and Mike teamed up at Marine Corps Base Camp Pendleton in Southern California in November 2002. Over the next year, they completed their training and certification as a patrol and

The Camp Pendleton military base in California has a facility for training dogs for deployment into Iraq and Afghanistan. The dogs and their handlers are trained for duties such as detecting explosives and narcotics and tracking suspects. Here, a dog learns to master a narrow bridgelike structure.

explosives detection dog (PEDD) team. A PEDD dog like Rex excels at guarding US military bases around the world from intruders. The dog also finds weapons, explosives, and bomb-making chemicals. Rex could catch and hold a suspect or enemy terrorist by chasing him, knocking him down, and clenching the person's clothing or a limb with his teeth. Few people resist when an aggressive 70-pound (32-kilogram) dog holds them down! The US military spends $50,000 or more to train a military working dog to this high level of excellence. By tradition, the military assigns these dogs a higher rank than their handlers to encourage the handler to treat their "superior officer" with the respect to which the dog is entitled.

OFF TO WAR

The Camp Pendleton kennel master—the soldier in charge of everything the dogs and their handlers need, including their medical care, feeding, and housing at a particular military base—told Mike and the other handlers in November 2003 that they would soon be deployed to Iraq. US military leaders realized that the nature of twenty-first-century warfare had changed from previous eras. No longer were armies dressed in different, identifiable uniforms. No longer were armies fighting each other openly on defined battlefields. Instead, US soldiers in the war in Iraq and in the war in Afghanistan (2001–2014) faced terrorists and enemy insurgents (rebels fighting against an established government). Typically these fighters wore civilian clothing and hid among local residents. From rooftops and distant hillsides, enemy snipers targeted American soldiers, whose desert camouflage outfits were distinctive. The enemy also built deadly improvised explosive devices (IEDs) and used them to injure and kill American soldiers. These devices, constructed of simple explosive materials, were usually hidden in rubble along roads, under bridges, or inside deserted houses.

Although the US military had used few dogs since the Vietnam War (1957–1975, with US involvement from early 1960s–1973), military leaders in the twenty-first century felt certain that trained dogs could save American lives in Iraq and Afghanistan by finding IEDs before they exploded. In 2004 Mike and Rex became one of the first handler-dog teams ever deployed to Iraq. "By trial and error, we're to learn how to take K9 units into the heart of war once again," Mike said.

Mike and Rex were ready for the challenge. Just before Mike and Rex left for Iraq, Mike's father, who had cancer, gave him a set of Irish rosary beads (used in Catholic prayers) to keep him safe. His mother, of Mexican Indian ancestry, gave him a small carved turquoise and black stone bear that symbolized protection.

When it was time to go, a giant transport airplane carried Mike, Rex, and eleven other handlers and dogs from March Air Reserve Base in Southern California to Iraq. The dogs rested in travel kennels in the center aisle of the plane, while their handlers sat nearby to comfort the dogs if they became agitated. The teams faced twenty-six hours in the air, with one stopover in the United States and another in Germany.

When the plane finally reached Iraq, it performed a military combat descent, a tight corkscrewing maneuver out of the dark night sky onto the airfield at Ayn al-Asad, Iraq. It took a few more days for Mike and Rex to reach their assignment at Mahmoudiyah, where marines were running into IEDs nearly every time they left camp and they, as well as civilians, were being wounded and killed. "It's a fact that 80 percent of those devices are killing innocent Iraqi civilians, mostly women and children," Mike said.

Mike and Rex were a team with a mission: to walk the very dangerous road known unofficially as IED Alley with bomb disposal experts. Following Mike and Rex, the men were to disarm any IEDs the team found to make the road safe for soldiers and jeeps. When Mike and Rex began each mission, Mike would show Rex his favorite toy—a nearly indestructible red rubber Kong. Mike remembers, "The moment Rex sees the Kong, he lowers his rump and sits at my feet, gazing lovingly at it. He knows we're moving into detection mode now. He knows if we don't find something he won't get to play with his beloved ball. I give him the command: Seek, seek, seek." Mike would then tuck the Kong back into his pocket, and the team was ready for the hunt.

"Rex lowers his head and goes to work, sifting the air expertly through his muzzle. This is a game to Rex, and one that he loves. His tail starts wagging, and he's smiling happily as he sets off on the search." When Rex would find the IED odor he had been trained to recognize, he would pause. His head would lift and the sniffing intensified. His tail would go up, and he would lower his head again to find the exact location of the suspicious odor. He would then get as close as possible to the source and stop. Rex would stare at the spot, then turn to look at Mike, saying in dog language that he had found something.

Mike and Rex would pull back while the bomb disposal experts moved in to defuse the bomb or to remove the explosive material. Meanwhile, Mike let Rex play with his Kong for a few moments as a reward. Dog handlers reward their dogs with praise and play instead of treats.

Despite the chaos of war and the nearly unbearable heat—temperatures can rise to 120°F (49°C) or more in this part of the Middle East—Rex found many IEDs and large amounts of bomb-making materials. Through this work, he saved Mike's life—and that of his fellow marines—numerous times.

MIKE AND REX WERE A TEAM WITH A MISSION: TO WALK THE VERY DANGEROUS ROAD KNOWN UNOFFICIALLY AS IED ALLEY WITH BOMB DISPOSAL EXPERTS.

One day, while searching an abandoned building in Zaidon, a tiny village outside of Fallujah, Iraq, Rex found a hoard of enemy weapons—AK-47s (a type of assault rifle) and machine guns. Later the same day, Mike and Rex searched the dusty edges of an irrigated field. When Rex would find something, he "shows a big change of behavior," Mike said. "We dig beneath where he's sat his butt on the earth, and presto, the Marines pull out a sack stuffed full of RPG [rocket-propelled grenade] warheads." The RPGs were new and shiny, 4 feet (1.2 meters) long, and were deadly to soldiers and innocent civilians alike.

On this mission, Mike picked up a warhead and posed with Rex for a photo. "[Rex's] eyes are glued to the warhead, with a shining light blazing out of them: *See, I got it! I got it!* He can't keep his gaze off [them]. They're his prize." Within hours the marines uncovered a ton (0.9 metric tons) or more of IED-making material, thanks to Rex.

The Iraqi insurgents targeted Mike and Rex because they were so good at finding hidden explosives. "The Iraqis hate Rex and me sniffing out all their weaponry. . . . We know the enemy is targeting our bomb-disposal guys. . . . It stands to reason that the more often they see Rex and me at work, the more they'll realize what K9 teams can do out here."

MIKE AND REX GO HOME

Mike and Rex finished their six-month tour in Iraq with only minor injuries. Mike's rosary shattered when he dived onto his chest during a battle one day. However, the Indian bear his mom gave him survived unbroken.

Mike and Rex returned to the United States, where they had a few more months together before Mike left the marines. On their last night together at Camp Pendleton, Mike fed Rex his dinner and then sat with him while Rex fell asleep, his head in Mike's lap. "In Iraq we put our lives in each other's hands (and paws) day after day. We took care of each other no matter what. Rex and I have a bond that will last for the rest of our born days."

Rex had nine handlers after Mike and two more tours of duty in Iraq. He performed flawlessly with each handler. Rex and Megan Leavey, one of Rex's later handlers, were both injured by an IED in Iraq in 2006. Both recovered. Mike had always wanted to adopt Rex. "When the process for Rex's adoption began, the Marine Corps called and gave me an opportunity to adopt him." But Mike felt that Megan should get Rex. "It was one of the toughest things I've ever done. . . . Despite how much I wanted to have Rex, it would have been wrong for me to get between a wounded warrior and the dog that could be her therapy for years to come."

At Rex's formal retirement ceremony at Camp Pendleton's K9 unit in 2012, a military official praised Rex's ten years as a MWD. The citation read in part, "MWD Rex performed his duties in an exemplary and highly professional manner. . . . MWD Rex's enthusiasm, initiative, and loyal devotion to duty reflected great credit upon himself, and were in keeping with the finest traditions of the Marine Corps and the United States Naval Service." A MWD handler then presented Rex's leash to Megan.

After Mike Dowling left the marines, he cofounded Veterans in Film and Television. He is also an author, actor, technical consultant, and public speaker.

MEGAN AND REX

Marine corporal Megan Leavey was one of the ten handlers with whom Rex worked during his career. Megan and Rex completed one hundred missions during their time together in Iraq in 2006. Their luck ran out when an IED exploded outside Ramadi in central Iraq. The explosion knocked Megan unconscious and damaged blood vessels inside her ears. All she could think about was Rex. "I remember waking up and pulling my leash and thinking, 'Oh, my God, please be something on the other end of this leash!'" Rex sustained a serious shoulder injury while Megan suffered a traumatic brain injury. Both Megan and Rex survived their injuries, although it took a year of recovery and rehabilitation for both of them to fully recover.

Megan was discharged in 2007 with a Purple Heart, a US military decoration awarded to soldiers wounded or killed during military service. The US Marines assigned Rex to a new handler. Megan tried for five years to adopt Rex. But the marines considered Rex such a valuable asset that they repeatedly denied her request. Rex developed paralysis of a facial nerve and became unable to work. The marines finally released him to Megan in April 2012.

By this time, Megan had been working as a security officer with a different dog at New York's Yankee Stadium. After Megan adopted Rex, the Yankees held a special ceremony for her at the stadium. Infielder Alex Rodriguez of the New York Yankees team presented Megan with a charm engraved with Rex's name. Rex died just a few short months later. "I am so grateful for the last eight months I got to spend with my partner and my best friend," Megan said. "Rex got to swim in a pool and play with my other dogs . . . sleep in a cozy bed next to me every night. He was one [heck] of a dog, one tough . . . Marine, and one very special soul."

Alex Rodriguez (*left*) greets former US Marine corporal Megan Leavey (*center*). Randy Levine (*right*), president of the New York Yankees, looks on during the May 2012 ceremony to honor Leavey and her MWD Rex (*on the leash*) at Yankee Stadium in New York.

Dowling remains very active in the veteran community, working with wounded warriors and veteran-related nonprofit organizations. He was awarded the US Navy and Marine Corps Achievement Medal for his service with Rex in Iraq.

WAR DOG TEAM IN VIETNAM: JOHN AND CLIPPER

"Directly to my front, Charlie opened up with automatic rifle and machine gun fire," John Burnam said, writing about an ambush that he and his dog Clipper lived through in 1967 when they served together in Vietnam. During this war, the United States and the South Vietnamese armies fought together to hold off the North Vietnamese, who wanted to unite the nation under Communist rule. Charlie was the American nickname for North Vietnamese enemy soldiers.

"Fortunately, I'd fallen near a small tree. I rolled behind it, Clipper at my side." John and Clipper were caught between the crossfire of his own men and the enemy. "Clipper and I lay only fifteen feet [4.5 m] from Charlie's entrenched positions. I could hear Vietnamese voices whispering from their foxholes. I knew Clipper heard them too, but he didn't make a sound. My dog and I were in deep [trouble] with no way out."

John Burnam joined the US Army in 1966 when he was eighteen years old. A few months after he celebrated his nineteenth birthday, the army sent him to fight in Vietnam. During one of his first battles, John jumped over a patch of elephant grass, fell, and immediately felt severe pain in his knee. "Looking down, I saw a yellow bamboo punji stake sticking right through my knee. It had

John Burnam and scout dog Clipper served together in Vietnam during the Vietnam War. Clipper saved Burnam's life many times but was left behind at the end of the war. Burnam never knew exactly what became of him.

entered under the kneecap and exited the other side." In Vietnam enemy soldiers planted these sharpened and often poisoned bamboo stakes in jungle booby traps. To treat this serious injury, the army sent John to the US Army General Hospital in Yokohama, Japan.

Early in 1967, after surgery and weeks of physical therapy, John reported to a huge American army supply depot on the island of Okinawa, part of the Ryukyu Islands lying to the south of Japan. Okinawa is a small island, and at the time, was heavily populated by all branches of the US military. The depot guarded ammunition storage buildings and serviced the American war effort in Vietnam. Because of John's injury, his superiors thought this would be a good place for him to serve the rest of his tour.

A personnel clerk assigned John to become a handler of sentry (guard) dogs, even though John had no experience working with dogs. "I liked the idea of having a dog of my own, even though it really belonged to Uncle Sam," he remembered. As John and one of the depot's dog handlers walked through the kennels where the dogs lived, each of the dogs lunged at John from its cage, growling and baring his teeth. "It didn't really matter which dog was assigned to me," John said, "because they all wanted to eat me. . . . Right then I feared every one of those dogs, and they sensed it."

The platoon sergeant asked John to work around the kennels for a few days to become familiar with dogs. He decided to assign John to Hans, a very large and strong-willed German shepherd. It took a few weeks for John and Hans to get acquainted. Once they were comfortable with each other, John and Hans trained together for another few weeks to become a sentry team. The sergeant assigned them to patrol a portion of the base where the US stored weapons, specifically underground structures called igloos, which were built of concrete and steel and then buried under dirt. Cages of rabbits sat atop vents on the igloos. John was told to check the rabbits frequently because the military stockpiled chemical warfare weapons deep beneath the igloos. If the rabbits looked sick or died, it signaled a possible leak of poison gas into the air. John carried two rubber gas masks, one for him and one for Hans to use if he tasted or smelled anything unusual in the air. "I must have practiced putting on my mask ten times that night," John said. "Hans was getting annoyed with the exercise, so I stopped when he started growling at me. *Hans, if you only knew! I thought."*

BACK TO VIETNAM

John and Hans worked well together, but after several months, John decided that he didn't want to spend any more time in Okinawa. He was bored and wanted to leave. He still owed the military another year of service, so he volunteered to return to combat in Vietnam. The army assigned John to an infantry combat unit although he'd wanted to be part of an air combat unit. Soon, however, came the opportunity he realized he'd been waiting for—an opening as a dog handler with the 44th Scout Dog Platoon.

At an American base built on the Michelin rubber plantation in the Vietnamese jungle, John teamed up with a young German shepherd named Timber. Weeks later, John and Timber came under enemy fire, and Timber was badly injured by shrapnel. Although he recovered physically, Timber was never the same. He lost his drive, his ambition, and his desire to work. John needed another dog.

So the army sent John to a US base in Saigon to find a new canine partner—his third. John walked along a string of kennels and stopped in front of one that held an 80-pound (36 kg) German shepherd with a black and brown coat and big brown eyes. The dog and John looked at each other and something clicked between them.

"If a dog could smile, Clipper smiled," John said. "He was friendly, playful, intelligent, and energetic. I just loved that dog. Clipper was not a pet. He was a soldier, a four-footed soldier. He was a working dog. He was smart, he obeyed commands, and he had the ability to learn things quickly." Clipper walked with a sense of pride and confidence, John thought. Like every US soldier, John wore dog tags around his neck as a form of identification. For dogs, the military tattooed ID numbers inside each dog's left ear. Clipper's number was 12X3.

In Vietnam, John and Clipper walked point, or led the way through enemy territory, one of the most dangerous jobs in Vietnam. "The enemy [which was hiding] usually had the advantage of spotting the American point man first," John said. "With a scout dog team, though, the tables were turned: we gained the advantage, because a dog's instincts, vision, and sense of smell and hearing were hundreds of times more acute than a human's. Clipper was like a walking radar beam."

The scout dog and his handler were the early warning system for the soldiers hiking behind them. John and Clipper led lines of US soldiers in a single file across fields, along trails, and through jungles. When Clipper smelled, heard, or saw something that worried him, he stopped and stared intensely and silently in the direction of danger. His ears stood tall, and his body tilted forward. When Clipper alerted like this, John knew something was wrong, and he warned his fellow soldiers by hand signals or whispered words that trouble lurked ahead.

Clipper allowed any American to pet him, but he had been trained to be aggressive toward the Vietnamese whether they were friend or enemy. Clipper became agitated and anxious around them, John said. "One reason was that the Vietnamese looked, talked, smelled, walked, and ate differently than Americans. Secondly, all the scout dogs were trained to hunt those characteristics, and were rewarded with love and affection when they found them. Besides, to keep the dogs from getting used to them, no Vietnamese were allowed inside the canine compound." On base, John and the other handlers used captured enemy clothing and weapons to train their dogs to alert on those smells.

> **"CLIPPER WAS NOT A PET. HE WAS A SOLDIER, A FOUR-FOOTED SOLDIER. HE WAS A WORKING DOG. HE WAS SMART, HE OBEYED COMMANDS, AND HE HAD THE ABILITY TO LEARN THINGS QUICKLY."**
>
> —JOHN BURNAM

In *A Soldier's Best Friend: Scout Dogs and Their Handlers in the Vietnam War*, the book John later wrote about his service in Vietnam, he describes how Clipper and other dogs saved his life and the lives of numerous other Americans many times. Mission after mission, the scout dogs warned American patrols of ambushes, snipers, and booby traps. John and Clipper worked together for nearly a

THE NOT FORGOTTEN FOUNTAIN

John Burnam worked tirelessly to establish the US Military Working Dog Teams National Monument at Lackland Air Force Base in San Antonio, Texas. The monument, built with donations raised by John Burnam's Memorial Foundation, was dedicated in 2013. Burnam also wanted a water fountain for dogs at the site. He felt it was imperative because dogs and their handlers would be visiting the monument. The Not Forgotten Fountain is built to the side of the larger monument and features a soldier pouring water into his helmet, a common way of providing water to dogs in the field.

Burnam kept Clipper and all the dogs left behind in Vietnam in his heart and mind for decades. In their memory, he wrote the inscription for the fountain: "In everlasting memory of all the heroic war dogs who served, died, and were left behind in the Vietnam War." The design of the fountain is based on a photo of John and Clipper (see page 12) in which Clipper rests his right foot on John's knee.

The Not Forgotten Fountain is part of a national monument in San Antonio to military war dogs. The fountain provides water for the dogs visiting the site.

"Not Forgotten Fountain"
"In everlasting memory of all the heroic war dogs who served, died, and were left behind in the Vietnam War.
–John Burnam, Vietnam Scout Dog Handler

year until his old punji stick knee injury started acting up. At twenty-one years old, John was discharged in 1968 and returned home to Colorado.

Clipper stayed in Vietnam and worked with other handlers until the Americans exited Vietnam hastily toward the end of the war in 1973. The army had no plans for bringing the dogs home or for smoothly transitioning them to new owners in Vietnam. Clipper would never go home. "This was not to be for the valiant war dogs of the Vietnam War," John said. "For their service, heroism, bravery under fire, and risking their lives to save others, the surviving dogs were given to the South Vietnamese army or disposed of by other means." He worried Clipper and the other dogs might be turned loose to forage for themselves in the jungle. He also knew that the Vietnamese people often ate dog meat, and that some of the dogs might end up in dog stew.

John described his final moments with Clipper. "The tragedy of it haunted me like a nightmare. . . . At last, the time had come for me to let go. I tried to hold back my tears. I didn't know how to say goodbye to my best friend, so I looked into his big brown eyes and gave him one last loving farewell bear hug. Then I turned and walked away awash in the sad bitter truth that Vietnam would become my dog's final resting place. . . . I truly had no more reason to stay in Vietnam, but every reason in the world to keep Clipper alive in my heart for the rest of my life."

Years later, John learned more about what might have happened to Clipper when the Americans left Vietnam. "This is the darkest chapter in the history of our nation's military working dog program," he said during an interview in 2015. "To have left the dogs behind in Vietnam in America's haste to leave was a tragedy of monumental consequences to them. To place the dogs in their shipping crates, load them on trucks, and turn them over to the South Vietnamese army without a proper transitional program was confusing and devastating to those magnificent and heroic dogs. I cried when I learned of this thirty years after I left my dogs Timber and Clipper alive in Vietnam in 1968. It still saddens me today."

John Burnam's two years of service in Vietnam earned him several awards, including a Purple Heart, Bronze Star, Legion of Merit medal, Meritorious Service Medal, and a Presidential Unit Citation, among others. He has devoted much of his life to advocating for military working dogs and their handlers. He was integral in founding the US Military Working Dog Teams National Monument and the Not Forgotten Fountain in memory of the Vietnam War dogs, both located at Lackland Air Force Base. Burnam is also an author, a speaker, and has appeared in several documentary films.

CHAPTER 2
THE DOGS OF WARS

Dogs have gone into battle alongside humans throughout history. Egyptian murals from four thousand years BCE depict soldiers unleashing dogs on enemies. The ancient Greeks and Romans also created wall paintings to record the exploits of war dogs. The paintings show dogs wearing spiked collars, chain mail armor, and padded jackets. Soldiers in ancient Britain used large mastiffs to fight the troops of Roman general Julius Caesar in 55 BCE. About 37 BCE, the Roman scholar Marcus Terentius Varro described what mastiffs should look like. "They should be comely of face [attractive], of good size, with eyes either darkish or yellowish . . . with two fangs projecting somewhat from [the upper lip] on the right and left, the upper straight rather than curved." Atilla, leader of the fierce central Asian nomads known as the Huns, used war dogs in battling the ancient

"Over the course of our nation's military history, more than one hundred thousand dogs of many different breeds faithfully served America. . . . Their deployment saved the lives of countless thousands of Americans, Allied troops, and noncombatants."

—Master Sergeant John C. Burnam (Retired), handler for Clipper during Vietnam War

Humans have long relied on dogs in hunting and in waging war. This wall panel from ancient Nineveh (a city in what later became northern Iraq) shows huntsmen with their hounds. The piece dates to about 645–635 BCE.

Roman Empire in the fifth century CE. William the Conquerer, king of England in the eleventh century CE, used war dogs as well.

Early war dogs didn't just fight. They carried supplies, pulled carts, and guarded camps. In the Middle Ages (about 500–1500 CE), soldiers trained dogs to carry deadly fire on their backs, run into enemy camps, shake off the fire, and dash back to their own troops.

When European explorers first reached the Americas in the 1400s, they brought war dogs with them. For example, Christopher Columbus brought dogs with him to Hispaniola (the island that in modern days is divided between the nations of Haiti and the Dominican Republic) in 1493, using them to disperse hostile

Indians. As they explored the North American continent, Spanish conquistadores such as Hernando de Soto, Juan Ponce de León, and Hernán Cortés also released huge dogs against indigenous populations to frighten them into submission or to subdue them in battle. Explorer Vasco Núñez de Balboa carried dogs with him as he crossed what is now Panama to the Pacific Ocean. He is said to have used them in 1513 to savagely attack and kill fifty Indians in the region.

In the United States, the US Army first used military dogs during the Second Seminole War (1835–1842), a war in which the US government fought the Seminole Indians over territory in Florida. The army relied on the dogs to track and capture Seminole Indians and runaway slaves in the dense swamps of Florida and Louisiana. In the Civil War (1861–1865), dogs served as messengers, guards, and mascots for both the Union army and the Confederate army. Often men took their own family dogs into battle with them. But it wasn't until after World War I (1914–1918) that the US military realized just how valuable trained war dogs could be.

DOGS IN WORLD WAR I

When the United States entered World War I in 1917, American military leaders didn't believe dogs would be of much help in the war effort. In fact, the United States was the only country fighting in the conflict that did not include working dogs in its military. By contrast, During World War I, Germany used about thirty thousand war dogs on the battlefields of Europe, while the French had at least twenty thousand. The British and Belgians had thousands more. Soldiers on both sides also used dogs to carry messages between base camps and the trenches that workers had dug into the mud on the front lines. Dogs cleared out rats from the trenches before soldiers settled in. Some dogs ferried baskets of pigeons on their backs. In combat conditions that were too dangerous for humans or dogs, the birds carried important messages between soldiers on the front lines and their commanders behind the lines.

During the war, each nation had its own version of what later became the Red Cross. The organizations provided trained "mercy dogs" to be used for the war effort. These dogs had one mission: to locate wounded soldiers and bring them medicine, food, and water. Often the dogs took a piece of the injured soldier's

World War I was the first conflict in which armies used chemical weapons, such as chlorine and mustard gas, on a large scale. Soldiers and their MWDs wore gas masks, specially developed to protect against the deadly impact of the gases. The German army was the first to deploy chemical weapons. This photo of German soldiers and their dogs dates to World War I.

clothing or his helmet to the medics at the dog's base camp and led the medics to the wounded man. Stories of these European war dogs reached Americans after the war and set the stage for US dogs to take part in future conflicts.

DOGS IN WORLD WAR II

What if the US government wanted your family's dog to sign up for the army? Would you let your dog go? That's what happened to thousands of pet dogs soon after the United States entered World War II (1939–1945) in 1941. The US military had no dogs trained to operate in war zones, so in early 1942, a group of Americans who worked with dogs started an organization called Dogs for Defense. These people knew that well-trained dogs could help American soldiers.

SERGEANT STUBBY

Stubby (*below right*) was the first true US war dog hero. The stub-tailed bull terrier wasn't drafted, nor did he enlist. Instead, Stubby wandered one day in 1917 into an outdoor army training session at Camp Yale, part of Yale University in New Haven, Connecticut. The soldiers who were training liked Stubby so much that they sneaked him aboard the transport ship SS *Minnesota* when they shipped off that same year to fight in France. Stowaway Stubby stuck to Corporal Robert Conroy, who became his unofficial handler. While serving eighteen months in Europe, Stubby participated in seventeen battles, even though he had no formal training as a war dog.

Soldiers during World War I used poisonous gas as a deadly weapon. Stubby saved his regiment from mustard gas numerous times by barking and nipping at soldiers in his unit when he smelled the slightest whiff of the deadly gas coming toward them. His behavior warned the men to put on their gas masks. Stubby even had his own gas mask.

Film celebrities of the time—including Greer Garson, Rudy Vallee, and Mary Pickford—donated their beloved pets to Dogs for Defense.

"Really, it was a sacrifice for so many citizens to give up their dogs for military service during World War II," army dog trainer Ralph Popp said in 2015. "For many people, I'm sure saying goodbye to their dogs was like saying goodbye to a son heading off to war . . . not knowing if they would ever return home." In all, Americans donated forty thousand dogs to the program. The military decided that about ten thousand of those dogs were suitable for training and returned the rest to their owners. The selected dogs had a tough time making the transition from

Bombs and shells were other typical armaments during this war. Yet the sound of shells whistling through the air didn't bother Stubby. The dog could hear the sound before the men could, and they learned to crouch down in the trenches when Stubby did. One fall night in 1918, at a huge battle in France's Argonne Forest, Stubby made history when he growled and bounded from the dugout where he had been sleeping next to Conroy. Conroy heard a pained shout and the sounds of a noisy scuffle. He jumped up and followed the sounds of the scuffle. He found Stubby holding a German enemy spy by the seat of his pants. The dog didn't let go of the flailing man until other soldiers arrived and took the spy into custody. No American dog had ever captured an enemy soldier before! In April 1918, a German shell fragment lodged in Stubby's leg during a major battle at Saint Mihiel in France. Doctors were able to save his life.

AN AMERICAN HERO

After the war, Stubby was introduced to three US presidents—Woodrow Wilson, Warren G. Harding, and Calvin Coolidge—and to General John J. Pershing, the US Army general who had led the United States and its allies to victory. Grateful soldiers bestowed medals and awards on Stubby, and the US Marines named him an honorary sergeant. American newspaper readers loved stories about Sergeant Stubby. He appeared in parades and other events. At a ceremony in Washington, DC, on July 6, 1921, held to honor veterans of the 102nd Infantry (the division with which Stubby served), General Pershing said Stubby was a "hero of the highest caliber." Stubby was the most famous animal in the United States after World War I until he died in 1926.

pampered pet to sentries, scouts, and mine detectors. But most of them made it through dog training camps in Virginia, Montana, Hawaii, and Mississippi and went on to serve their country.

During the war, army dog trainers narrowed the types of dogs that would be accepted to serve to seven breeds: German shepherds, Dobermans, Belgian sheepdogs, collies, Siberian huskies, malamutes, and Eskimo dogs. These larger dogs were better suited both physically and temperamentally for the hardships of training and battlefield conditions. Americans whose dogs were too small for the military could instead buy a rank for their pooch: one dollar to make your dog an

Trixie, a shepherd MWD, loved flying. Here, Staff Sergeant John W. Patrick adjusts her parachute harness at Fort Benning, Georgia, during World War II after the dog had made a landing during training. Parachuting dogs were sometimes called paradogs.

honorary private, and one hundred dollars for the rank of general. The money paid for training war dogs.

In the early days of the war, the dogs guarded beaches and military facilities in the United States to prevent sabotage (deliberate destruction) and to prevent spies from sneaking into these sites. Military leaders soon decided to move the dogs to war zones overseas. Dogs worked alongside soldiers in the fields and forests of European battlefields. In the Asian theater of the war, US Marines deployed dogs on Pacific islands to sniff out Japanese enemy positions. Dogs were especially helpful in the difficult jungle terrain of those islands. During a fierce battle between the Americans and Japanese in the Solomon Islands in 1943, US soldiers sent reports back to headquarters about two dogs. "On the first day of the battle, Andy (a Doberman pinscher) led M Company all the way to the road block. He alerted them to scattered sniper [positions], and undoubtedly was the means of preventing loss of life." On the second day of battle, the enemy cut M Company's phone lines, and a German shepherd named Caesar was the only means of communication. "Caesar was wounded . . . and had to be carried back to [camp] on a stretcher, but he had already established himself as a hero," the report read.

US military working dogs saved an estimated fifteen thousand US soldiers in World War II. At the end of the war, military leaders kept their promise to return the borrowed dogs who had survived the war to their owners. After awarding each dog an honorable discharge, the US government paid for the cost of shipping the dogs back home. Most of the dogs in the Dogs for Defense program were reunited with their families or retired with their military handlers.

Mrs. Edward Jo Conally of Utah, had loaned her dog to the US military.

Starting in 1944, US Marine dog platoons conducted thousands of patrols throughout the Pacific islands during World War II. Lieutenant Clyde A. Henderson commanded the First War Dog Platoon, and they served with the 2nd Raider Battalion on Bougainville Island (*pictured above*) in Papua New Guinea.

THE DOGS OF WARS

CHIPS

Even a mutt can be a war hero. Chips was a mix of German shepherd, Siberian husky, and collie. He lived with the Edward Wren family in New York. Chips was very protective of the family's children. After he bit a local man, Wren decided Chips's aggressive nature should be used for the good of the country, and he donated Chips to the military's Dogs for Defense Program. After Chips completed his training in 1942, the US Army sent him to Europe with handler Private John P. Rowell.

During World War II, enemy soldiers on European battlefields often killed sentries who guarded American camps at night. When Chips and other military dogs joined sentry teams, the canines alerted their handlers when strangers approached. This gave the soldiers time to react quickly, and no soldier on guard duty with a MWD died after the dogs joined the teams. Chips and his handler served in North Africa, France, Germany, and Italy, where Chips attacked a dugout filled with Italian gunners. Even though Chips took a bullet himself, he seized one enemy soldier and forced four others to surrender by shoving them out of the gunners' nest.

Grateful soldiers awarded the Silver Star (a medal awarded for bravery in action against an enemy of the United States) and a Purple Heart to Chips. The US Army later revoked the awards, saying it was demeaning to human soldiers to give medals to animals. Chips is also famous for biting General Dwight D. Eisenhower, Supreme Commander of European Allied Forces, when the general bent over to give him a congratulatory pat in 1943.

MWD Chips sits for a doughnut treat from an American soldier during World War II. In 1943 Chips attacked a gunners' nest in Sicily (an island off the coast of Italy) and took down several enemy soldiers, forcing the men to surrender. Chips was the most decorated MWD of World War II.

She wrote to the quartermaster general (the army officer in charge of supplies, including dogs), "Thank you for your good care and training of our dog Mike. He knew all of us and still remembers the tricks he knew before he entered the service. My son, Edward, an Army officer, and all of us are proud of [Mike's] honorable discharge and his deportment." Dogs proved their value to the US military in World War II, and since then, the military has owned and trained war dogs for every conflict in which the United States has engaged.

DOGS IN THE KOREAN WAR

The US military scaled back its working dog program after World War II so that only one platoon of eighteen handlers and twenty-seven dogs—mostly German shepherds—remained in the army. The army sent the dogs and their handlers to South Korea when the United States and South Korea were fighting North Korean troops in the Korean War (1950–1953). The primary job of the dog teams was to scout enemy soldiers on the battlefield and to protect American troops. Many

More than fifteen hundred MWDs served alongside US troops in the Korean War. These dogs served in the field in South Korea, working as scouts with US soldiers from the 26th Infantry Scout Dog Platoon. The photo dates to June 1951.

THE DOGS OF WARS

North Korean soldiers had never seen such large, fearsome dogs. They often tried to shoot them first, before aiming at American soldiers. The North Korean army frequently broadcast propaganda during the night over loudspeakers set up on the North Korean side of the battlefield to try to unnerve the American soldiers. One night the loudspeakers blared, "Yankee—take your dog and go home!"

About fifteen hundred dogs served in the Korean War, and they excelled at their jobs. The US Army estimated that these MWDs reduced casualties by 65 percent in the parts of Korea where they served. At the end of the Korean War, the US military reassigned the dogs to US military bases around the globe, where they served as sentry dogs. In 1953 the US Army cited the dogs and their handlers for their service in Korea, saying: "The 26th Infantry Scout Dog Platoon is cited for exceptionally meritorious conduct in the performance of outstanding services in direct support of combat operations in Korea during the period 12 June 1951 to 15 January 1953."

WAR DOGS OF VIETNAM

Meanwhile, war was raging between the French and the Vietnamese in Southeast Asia. The United States did not send ground troops to Vietnam until 1965. The United States aided the South Vietnamese in the conflict with the North Vietnamese for eight years. The US military sent the first MWDs to Vietnam in 1965 for a test run. No one was sure if the dogs could adapt to the hot, humid climate and the jungle terrain in that part of the world. The dogs adapted very well and did an outstanding job at whatever duties their military handlers assigned to them. They also did well in the nontraditional guerrilla warfare of this conflict, in which enemy soldiers were often impossible to see and battles were fought in unpredictable conditions and at unexpected times and places.

Most of the military dogs that worked in Vietnam were German shepherds. They were chosen for their even temperament and their adaptability to new environments and people. "Their intimidating size allowed them to take a man down quite easily, and they could be trained to be aggressive for sentry duty or to be passive for scouting," said John Burnam, who worked with German shepherds in Vietnam. "They could adapt to changing from one handler to another in a short

Muzzled sentry dogs and their handlers return to their base camp near the coastal city of Da Nang, South Vietnam, in 1969. The team had finished a patrol of the perimeter of a US Navy supply and communications outpost in the area.

time." Burnam said. "A dog's senses, coupled with his loyalty and desire to serve a master, make him invaluable as a scout."

Dogs filled several roles in Vietnam:

1. Scout dog teams consisted of one German shepherd and one handler. "A scout dog was designed to lead the patrol out and use his natural senses to find the enemy before the enemy found us," Burnam said. These teams served as the eyes and ears of American patrols, looking for ambushes, snipers, hidden weapon caches, and trip wires rigged to explosives. Some dogs could hear the very faint sound of wind blowing across wires, which were nearly invisible to soldiers.

2. Tracker teams were made up of a Labrador retriever (sometimes a German shepherd), a handler, and two to three other men. These teams tracked by sight and scent (blood and body odor) to locate missing or injured American soldiers (such as downed pilots) or to find enemy soldiers.

THE DOGS OF WARS

3. Sentry or patrol dog teams—one German shepherd and one handler—protected US military bases, weapons depots, and other strategic areas from enemy infiltrators. According to the US War Dogs Association, a group founded by Ron Aiello to support and honor all war dogs and their handlers, most of the sentry teams worked at night with a mission to "Detect, Detain, and Destroy."

4. Water dogs rode in American war boats to patrol rivers. The dogs learned to detect enemy soldiers hidden under the water. The soldiers could stay for long periods under the water by breathing through hoses, snorkels, or hollow reeds.

Burnam wrote about US military dogs in Vietnam, "Mission after mission . . . scout dogs alerted American patrols of ambushes, snipers, and booby traps. . . . The enemy tried to counteract the scout-dog teams' success by offering rewards to any soldier that killed scout dogs and their handlers." North Vietnamese leaders offered bounties of 20,000 US dollars or more to soldiers who killed an American military dog. The bounty for killing an American dog handler was only half that much. To receive the bounty money, a North Vietnamese soldier had to turn over the tattooed ear of an American MWD or the US military K9 patch from a slain soldier's uniform showing that he was a dog handler.

Military dogs in Vietnam often filled another role, one that came naturally to them. "My dog was also my therapist," said Aiello, who patrolled in Vietnam with his beloved German shepherd, Stormy, for thirteen months. "I could talk to her about anything." Other soldiers appreciated her as well. After a deadly exchange [of gunfire] with the enemy, they would reach out to hug or pat Stormy. "You could see the tension drain from their face. She probably reminded them of a dog back home," Aiello remembers.

In all, an estimated ten thousand soldiers and about four thousand dogs worked as teams in Vietnam, faithfully performing everything asked of them. The Vietnam Veterans Memorial in Washington, DC, holds the names of more than fifty-eight thousand Americans killed in Vietnam. "Without [the dogs], there would have been another ten thousand names on the Wall," Aiello said. He added that Stormy saved his life and those of other soldiers "more times than I could count."

NEMO

Nemo and his handler, Airman Bob Thorneburg, detected several enemy soldiers who had penetrated the boundary of an American air base in Vietnam in December 1966. When Thorneburg saw the soldiers, he told Nemo to "Get him," the command to charge and attack the enemy. Nemo lunged forward, with Thorneburg close behind. In seconds Thorneburg killed two of the enemy soldiers. Then two bullets struck Thorneburg. Another bullet hit Nemo in the eye, and several others hit him in the face.

Nemo continued to fight, giving Thorneburg time to radio his position to fellow American soldiers nearby before he passed out from blood loss. Despite Nemo's severe injuries, he returned to Thorneburg and crawled over his handler's body, guarding him against further attack until medical help arrived.

Nemo lost his right eye but recovered from all his other injuries, as did Thorneburg. Nemo was one of the few MWDs to return from Vietnam. He became a symbol of canine heroism and retired to a kennel at Lackland Air Force Base, where he lived in style until his death at the age of eleven.

MWD Nemo lost his right eye from a bullet wound as he fought off North Vietnamese enemy soldiers in 1966. He guarded his wounded handler, Bob Thorneburg *(left)*, during the fire exchange that injured them both.

Dogs showed their ability to protect their handlers and other soldiers over and over again. "Without Toro, I wouldn't have made it back to the States," Specialist Carl Dobbins said of his dog. "In fact, I wouldn't have made it three months without Toro."

Most of the dog handlers serving in Vietnam didn't realize the US military viewed the MWDs as government property. Military officials felt it would be too expensive to transport the dogs back home after a tour of duty and that it was unlikely the dogs could be integrated into civilian life after their military training. "We were all so attached to these dogs, these animals. They had feelings, they hurt, they cried, they got sad, they got happy," Sergeant Spencer Dixon, handler for a MWD named Shack, said. "They saved a lot of boys' lives."

Only about two hundred of the MWDs that served in Vietnam returned to the United States. Handlers tried to bring their dogs back home, but US military leaders would not allow it. Instead, they ordered veterinarians and technicians in Vietnam to euthanize hundreds of loyal dogs. Burnam later wrote, "The rest of the brave Vietnam war dogs were . . . given to the South Vietnamese army, which meant, given Vietnamese cultural practices, that the dogs might have been slaughtered for food."

About leaving his dog, Wolf, behind, Specialist Charlie Cargo of the 48th Scout Dog Platoon said, "It was just like somebody ripped out my heart . . . It was probably the hardest thing I ever did in my life."

ROBBY'S LAW

Up until 2000, few dogs were reunited with their handlers or other families after they left the military. Instead, the dogs continued to work until they developed medical problems. When they could no longer work, the military euthanized them. The military euthanized about two hundred dogs a year in the late 1990s. That policy changed on November 6, 2000, when President Bill Clinton signed a law known as Robby's Law that said whenever possible, MWDs were to be returned to civilian life. Law enforcement agencies, former handlers, and other people capable of caring for retired MWDs were allowed to adopt the animals.

Robby's Law came about when Congressman Roscoe Bartlett of Maryland read about the Defense Department's policy of euthanizing war dogs in the September 2000 issue of *Stars and Stripes* magazine. The article also mentioned a US Marine Corps dog named Robby, who was sick and near the end of his career. Knowing that Robby could be euthanized, Bartlett visited a MWD demonstration at Marine Corps Base Quantico in Virginia. He watched one dog chase and capture a suspect. But when it came time for Robby to do his part, he failed. Although only eight years old, the Belgian Malinois suffered from bad hips, arthritis, and a growth in his spine.

Bartlett met with Robby's handler, Lance Corporal Shawn Manthey, who wanted desperately to adopt Robby. Instead, the military sent Robby to Lackland to become a training dog. Bartlett pushed for Robby's Law, but when it passed in November 2000, Manthey and his wife were expecting a baby. He could not adopt Robby because he couldn't afford the expensive medication that Robby needed. Robby lived out the last few months of his life at Lackland.

In February 2001, Robby received a hero's funeral at the nation's first pet cemetery in New York. Beverly Gainer, keynote speaker at the funeral, said, "We don't know how many lives have been saved by these dogs, how many terrorists attempts have been prevented because bombs were sniffed out by dogs. The minimum we can do for anyone who gives his life in service of the country and saving human lives is to give them the opportunity to have a few restful years and burial."

CHAPTER 3
THE RIGHT DOG FOR THE JOB

Most American companion dogs live comfortable, healthy lives. They have food, toys, affection, health care, and plenty of time to play and exercise. They are happy and behave well. However, some dogs sit at home on the couch or in the backyard for many hours, alone and bored, waiting for their people to come home. That boredom may lead to anxiety and to destructive or dangerous behaviors. Some dogs have jobs—real jobs that give their lives purpose. They herd sheep, pull sleds, and find lost children. They detect illegal drugs and termites and are even used to detect some kinds of cancer, just by the odor of a patient's breath. If the dogs work with the police, they help catch criminals. These working dogs love their work, and they don't demand any payment for the jobs they do.

Military working dogs have jobs too. And their handlers say the

"There is the dog that is the fine animal that is useful for military working dog service. But there is a quality of dog above that . . . the dog whose drive is stronger, whose nerves are stronger and whose courage is higher."

—Stewart Hilliard, chief of MWD breeding, Lackland Air Force Base, Texas

Staff Sergeant Christa Quam holds her puppy, which has passed its puppy evaluation at Lackland Air Force Base. It will enter the military working dog program with the base's 341st Training Squadron when it is about seven months old.

animals love their work. The dogs work hard, play hard, and seem to enjoy every minute of it. They don't understand the concept of the danger they may face, yet they serve faithfully. To the dogs, it's all about doing their assigned jobs to the best of their ability, chasing toys, and getting praise and love from their handlers. It all starts with puppies born from top-notch parents with proven abilities.

PUPPIES: THE EARLY DAYS

Nearly all MWDs, whether destined for the army, navy, air force, or marines, receive at least part of their training at Lackland Air Force Base. Lackland is the only US facility that trains dogs for military use. In 1998 the US Department of Defense started a breeding program at Lackland with the goal of ultimately providing the US military with one-third of the MWDs needed each year. Currently, about 85 percent of all military dogs come from European breeders known for producing high-quality dogs. The Lackland training facility produces about 15 percent of the dogs, according to Stewart Hilliard, chief of MWD evaluations and breeding at Lackland, and a behavioral neuroscientist with decades of experience in breeding and training dogs.

While the US military uses several breeds of MWDs, most are Belgian Malinois and German shepherds. Lackland breeds only Belgian Malinois, using carefully selected parents with healthy genetic lines. Hilliard notes that "the breed suffers from fewer genetically-based medical problems than does the other possible breed for us—German shepherds—with lower rates of hip dysplasia [an abnormal formation of the hip socket], and elbow and spinal problems." Lackland followed the example of a top police dog breeding program in Germany. Hilliard says, "The program experienced a 16 or 17 percent increase in success rates when we switched from German shepherds to Malinois due to fewer medical problems and higher pass rates in character testing."

The Malinois breed has proven to produce outstanding MWDs that can carry out their missions well whether on an American military base or in a foreign

Puppies in Lackland's puppy program are frequently evaluated to see if they will be suited for the base's MWD program when they are older.

combat zone. The dogs are slightly smaller than German shepherds and have shorter hair, making them a bit easier to care for. Belgian Malinois are intelligent and trainable and have a strong desire to work and to please their handlers. Hilliard describes two of his best breeding females, RRespect and UUkita. (Dogs bred at Lackland always have names that begin with double capitalized letters to set them apart from other MWDs.) "What's special about RRespect and UUkita is they come from a very strong family," he said. "When you look at their brothers and sisters, many of them are high-quality dogs." These dogs, "when bred properly, will produce more high-quality dogs."

The DoD describes the Lackland breeding program like this on its Facebook page: "From birth to eight weeks our pups are reared at the Military Working Dog Center on Lackland [Air Force Base] in our state-of-the-art whelping facility [the building where dogs give birth]. While there is no guarantee that any pup of this age will develop into an adult working dog, our Puppy Development Specialists begin working with the pups from birth, imprinting and exposing the pups to a variety of stimulations and activities that will prepare them for the next phase of their life."

Human interaction begins when the puppies are three days old to quickly accustom them to being handled. Training assistants play with the puppies to get a feel for their personalities. When the puppies are a few weeks old, they go through their first aptitude test to determine if they have what it takes to become a MWD. For example, a puppy that passes this test approaches people with its tail held high, which demonstrates friendliness and confidence. Sniffing out hidden puppy treats shows a determination to hunt. The puppy that does not struggle when held on its back displays trust, a required trait. It will chase and return a ball with enthusiasm. A love of toys is another sign that a puppy can become a good MWD because toys are essential to training and rewarding MWDs.

PUPPIES IN PARADISE

Once the puppies are six to eight weeks old and have passed the aptitude test, they leave the base to go home with foster parents from the San Antonio area. "Families love to do it," said Bernadine Green, who works with the Lackland breeding program. "It's their way of giving back to the community and the military, and also for the sheer pleasure of caring for a puppy. This phase is probably the most [important] part of the program." She adds that having foster parents raise puppies makes for well-rounded dogs.

Lora Harrist and her family started fostering MWD puppies in 2013. After caring for seven puppies, Lora is an experienced puppy foster parent. "Before we started fostering, we had no experience with the Belgian Malinois, so we did lots of research on them. They are extremely intelligent, high-drive, problem-solving dogs, which makes them great working dogs. Little did we know we would fall in love with the breed," she says. Belgian Malinois puppies are so active and so driven that "some foster parents nickname them malligators because the dogs clack their jaws like alligators when playing or catching something in the air."

OOsceola lived with the Harrist foster family as part of his training. Foster families socialize their puppies so they will be comfortable with a wide range of people and places.

The main job of foster parents during the time they have the dogs is socialization. "It's important for the puppies to learn at an early age to be comfortable in new environments and to meet new people," Lora says. "We take the puppies as many places as we can, such as restaurants, stores, and even hockey games. Our first puppy SSheila was lucky enough to meet Taylor Swift and give her kisses!" Other puppies fostered with the Harrist family have included TTara, FFarah, and OOsceola. Then there's DDexter. "He's a Dutch shepherd that we adopted because he decided military life was not his thing," Lora says.

TIME FOR PUPPY SCHOOL

The next step begins when the foster puppies are about seven months old. Experts again evaluate the pups to be sure they're ready to enter training school at Lackland. If they are, foster families return the pups to the base. This can be a tough transition for foster parents and puppies. Families may grieve for the loss of the puppy they've come to love. Puppies must adjust to sleeping alone in a kennel instead of on a soft bed or with a special person in a home.

Fostering puppies is not for everyone. "It's not easy to give up the puppy at seven months. When we foster these dogs, our whole lives revolve around them," Lora says. "They're like children to us in many ways. We do everything we can to give them the tools to be strong, confident, loving partners that will protect their handlers and do their jobs. When it's time for the puppies to "report for duty" as we call it, it's a sad, yet proud day. To watch the pup that we've raised grow from a clumsy ball of fluff into a confident and regal dog marching off to the [Lackland] kennels fills your heart with such pride. Your baby is going to go out there and will save lives so that someone else's loved ones will be kept safe and make it back home."

Puppies that can't make the transition from home life to training are not suitable for military work. And those that don't do well in the program for any reason at any time are put up for adoption. In fact, the majority of the dogs available for adoption through Lackland are dog-school dropouts. They were not suited to complete the rigorous training required of a MWD. They go up for adoption at a young age—usually less than two years old. Foster parents generally get the first chance to adopt a puppy they raised. If they cannot take the puppy, it will go to someone else on the long list of people waiting to adopt.

The next phase of training at Lackland—puppy boot camp—lasts several months and is preparation for the actual MWD training. Pups learn to hunt for toys and to obey simple voice commands and hand signals such as sit and stay. Obedience is vital. A dog that does not completely obey its trainer could put both animal and human in danger once they are in a real war zone. Trainers also expose the puppies to loud noises such as aircraft engines and gunfire, which they will encounter in a combat zone. The dogs are trained to become used to being in large, loud military vehicles and in strange buildings. They also learn to wind their way through tunnels and across elevated steps. This phase of preparation lasts until the dogs are about twelve months old.

Specialists then evaluate the puppies for entry into the 341st Training Squadron's MWD training program at Lackland. Hilliard says there are three instinctive drives that demonstrate a puppy's potential to become a MWD. "First, the dogs must have a strong predatory drive. Also called prey drive, this behavior is especially important for search dogs and bomb-detecting dogs. We harness their inborn motivation, their instinct to chase stuff that moves, to pick it up, and to hold it in their mouths—sort of a modified hunting dog behavior. We want a lot of this drive for drug and bomb detection dogs. We train the dogs to search for the odor [drug or bomb] and to associate it with the reward—usually a ball or Kong."

The other two drives that predict a successful MWD are the bite drive and environmental stability. "The bite drive is not exactly aggression, but the need to grab stuff and hold on. Dogs with a strong bite drive love to play tug of war," Hilliard says. "This drive is vital for patrol dogs that chase, catch, and hold on to a fleeing suspect. We want a dog that bites with a full mouth, which is stronger and more powerful than a dog that bites with just a few teeth. Lastly, dogs with strong environmental stability are confident and bold. They have steady nerves and will act like themselves no matter where they are. New environments, scary noises, or strange people do not intimidate environmentally stable dogs."

Lackland does not breed the majority of MWDs, so many of them arrive from other breeders and kennels in Europe when they are at least one year old. After evaluation at Lackland, trainers slot the pups into the training program that fits their developmental and skill levels. Some dogs are more advanced and can skip the early stages of formal training, while others start at the beginning. For example, some dogs may not understand English at first, so trainers at Lackland start out giving commands to the dogs in languages they understand, such as German or Czech, before moving into English-language commands. About one-

Lance Corporal Mathew Weah and his MWD, Dixie, train in a field in Hartsville, South Carolina.

tenth of European dogs that come to Lackland for preparatory MWD training do not successfully complete the program and are offered to civilian police forces, are used to train new handlers, or are adopted out to civilian families.

RUNNING WITH THE BIG DOGS

Once puppies demonstrate required drives and traits, staffers at Lackland's MWD program begin their work. They perform specialized training over the next four months. The dogs first learn how to patrol and how to catch and detain people. MWDs don't chase and bite people because they are vicious animals. They do it to please their handlers and to obtain their favorite toys as rewards. During training, staff role-plays as enemy soldiers. They wear padded suits or a padded sleeve to protect them when the dog launches itself at them like a small missile going about 30 miles (48 kilometers) per hour. The protective padding is necessary because German shepherds and Belgian Malinois can bite just about as hard as lions and great white sharks!

A US Army soldier engages in tug-of-war training with an MWD at a military base in southern Afghanistan in 2010. Trainers work with a dog's instinctive predatory and bite drives, which are especially important to develop for chasing and catching enemy suspects.

Most MWDs are trained for two jobs, either patrol and IED detection *or* patrol and narcotics detection, never both. The potential for confusion and even injury or death would be too great if a dog searched for both drugs and explosives. The handler would have no way of knowing whether the dog found a stash of cocaine or a pile of explosives. Cocaine does not injure the dog or handler, while an IED is potentially deadly to anyone standing nearby if it goes off. When a dog is trained to detect *either* drugs or IEDs, the handler knows immediately what the dog has alerted to—drugs or explosives. The handling and disposition of each is very different. If a dog finds drugs, the handler is allowed to dig them up. However, if a dog finds an IED, the handler relies on bomb disposal experts to dig up and disarm the explosive.

Searching for drugs or explosives is an extension of a dog's early training of searching for toys. Trainers introduce different drug scents to the dogs and then hide the drugs in rooms, clothing, mail, and cars, for example. In one common exercise, a handler hides 1 ounce (28 grams) of cocaine or marijuana in a large military cargo plane. A well-trained dog can find the drug within a minute or two of boarding the plane, despite the overwhelming smell of aircraft fuel, hydraulic fluid, and other distracting odors.

In the case of IEDs, the dogs learn to recognize the scents of nine or more dangerous chemicals commonly used to make bombs. As with drug detection, trainers hide materials with the scents of chemicals and explosives in different environments, such as houses, markets, and bomb-making labs. The Lackland facility has created simulated versions of these environments to closely resemble the real-world experience. Dogs receive rewards of praise and toys when they find the hidden drugs or explosive scents.

"Dogs already know how to search for things," said Lillian Hardy, who worked with the US Department of Homeland Security at Indiana's Camp Atterbury. "For us, it's just teaching the dog how to scent [smell] what we're looking for, and for them, they have to learn how to tell us that they've found it."

Dogs alert their handlers when they find something important. Dogs naturally alert (or may be trained to alert) in individual ways to the odors of drugs or explosives. For example, Burnam's dog Clipper stopped moving and stared in the direction of danger with his ears standing tall and his body tilted forward. Mike Dowling's dog Rex moved as close as possible to the IED source, stared at the spot, then looked back and forth between Dowling and the spot where he smelled explosives. Other dogs may sit, stand, twitch their ears, and look to the handler for further instructions.

However, not all the dogs that make it this far (one to two years old) end up serving in the military. According to the DoD's MWD Facebook page, dogs that don't meet the DoD's requirements may be assigned to work for the Transportation Security Administration, the federal agency that protects US airports, or for US law enforcement agencies throughout the United States. Others, such as Lora Harrist's dog DDexter, leave the program early because they are not suitable to military work and may be adopted by foster parents or handlers.

When the dogs are two years old, they are assigned to their first handler. Staff Sergeant Sharif DeLarge, who works with MWD OOlaf, says, "He is an agile, fast, strong, and hard-hitting dog. His detection capabilities are spot on, which is essentially the most important job he has as a military working dog. . . . OOlaf's desire to please me as his handler is especially exceptional when it comes to any task I give him."

A TRIP TO THE OPERATING ROOM

All MWDs make a quick trip to the operating room just as they finish training at Lackland. While under general anesthesia, veterinarians tattoo each dog's identification number inside the left ear. Female dogs are spayed because a female dog in heat will attract male dogs for mating. Male dogs are not neutered because military trainers believe that their surging hormones make them more aggressive and generally better at their jobs.

All dogs over 35 pounds (16 kg) also undergo a potentially lifesaving procedure called a gastropexy to prevent bloating. Bloating is a dangerous medical condition that can happen when a large dog eats or drinks too rapidly after exercise. The stomach fills with gas and twists into loops, cutting off oxygen and blood supply to the stomach and intestines. The bloated stomach can press against the lungs and even the heart. Dogs can go into shock and die a painful death within hours if they don't receive emergency treatment. To prevent this complication, the surgeon stitches the stomach wall to the abdominal wall during the operation so the stomach cannot twist or shift. Before surgeons began performing this procedure on all large MWDs, about 9 percent of dogs died from bloat. Dogs recover quickly from these procedures and are ready to move on to the next phase of training or into military service.

ADVANCED TRAINING

According to Lisa Rogak, who has written about MWDs, by graduation time, the dogs are "lean, mean, attacking machines who usually only bond with one person—their handler—and come to view any other two-legged being as the enemy or, at the very least, someone to be wary of."

After graduation, dogs may be paired at Lackland with the handler with whom they will work in the field. More often, the Lackland program sends well-trained dogs to US military bases around the country that have requested dogs. Sometimes handlers, trainers, or kennel masters that have requested a MWD will come to Lackland to get to know the dog before bringing it back to their base. Regardless of how a MWD and its handler meet, feeding, grooming, exercise, and play help the pair bond over the course of their time together.

Kennel masters say the dogs and their handlers often share similar personality traits. "Dogs, just like people, have very distinct personalities," Sergeant Paul Baldwin, kennel master at Utah's Hill Air Force Base, says. "So we try to pair the right dogs with the right handlers so it's a good fit on both sides." For example, dogs and humans can be outgoing or more laid-back. Assigning a bold, aggressive dog to a quiet, mild-mannered handler may not be a good match. Instead, a high-energy dog is best matched to a high-energy, outgoing handler. Most MWDs are alpha dogs—a dog that is a natural leader and that will dominate and lead a pack of other dogs, if given the chance. In a good working military relationship, it must be clear from the beginning that the human handler is always the alpha (much like any human-dog relationship).

After pairing up, most MWDs that have been trained to detect IEDs and their handlers (from all branches of the military) travel to Yuma Proving

US Air Force technical sergeant Harvey Holt and his MWD, Jackson, search for weapons in Khan Bani Saad, a town to the north of Iraq's capital city, Baghdad. MWDs are carefully trained to detect explosives and other weapons at Yuma Proving Ground in Arizona before they are deployed overseas.

Ground in Arizona, about an hour's drive from the city of Yuma. The intense three-week training program prepares the MWDs for deployment into a war zone. The teams—dressed in full combat gear—work both day and night in the hot desert environment there, learning how to search for IEDs in mocked-up houses built of mud and clay, mosques (Islamic houses of worship), and roads built to resemble the environments the teams will face when deployed to the Middle East. In fact, the training site was modeled after a satellite image of a real village in Iraq.

Some dog-handler teams train as specialized IED search teams in which the dogs learn to work off the leash. In real-world battle zones, off-leash dogs can typically search for explosives more quickly and efficiently than can leashed dogs. An unleashed dog also works farther in front of its handler than a leashed dog. If the off-leash dog encounters an IED, the human is at less risk of injury should the device explode.

A few specialized tracker teams go through training at Yuma each year as well. Tracker teams were widely used in the Vietnam War. However, twenty-first-century military equipment, such as camera-equipped unmanned drones, can do much of what tracker teams once did. That means that fewer tracker teams are needed. Dogs searching for IEDs are familiar with a given number of chemical and explosive smells. Tracker dogs follow different odors—the odor of a fleeing suspect or enemy soldier—every time they go to work.

Training has its light moments as the dogs learn to deal with distractions. For example, choruses of coyotes howl in the darkness at Yuma. And a nearby rancher brings in a variety of animals—camels, horses, sheep, goats, cows, donkeys, chickens, and a goose—two days a month. "Having the animals here is all about creating natural distractions [for the dogs]," says Ben Standley of the Camel Farm near Yuma. "Military working dogs have to be able to discriminate between scents around them and not be distracted by the noise [and smell] of animals." The ranch animals and dogs tolerate each other, but the goose is mean and often acts aggressively toward the dogs, Standley says. The dogs must learn to focus on their handlers' commands and to ignore other animals they may encounter, whether at Yuma or in a Middle Eastern war zone.

BY SEA AND AIR

After completing advanced training at Yuma, dogs and handlers return to their bases. If they aren't immediately deployed, handlers work with their MWDs every day, both to maintain the tight bond between them and to keep the dogs' skill levels high. There's always something new to learn. For example, Corporal Suzette Clemans and her MWD, Denny, have trained on amphibious (land and water) landing craft air cushions (LCACs) at a beach near Camp Pendleton. "The LCAC is basically a hover craft that goes over water and lands on the beach," she says. "It's good training because the dog goes from being on a vessel to working right on the beach. Some dogs can get nervous inside tight spaces [of the LCAC], the waves might make them feel sick or uncomfortable, and getting on and off the vessel can be stressful for them." While LCACs are big enough to hold trucks and other military equipment, dogs and humans must ride in a small room with only two tiny windows.

Some dogs even learn to parachute. The military is reluctant to say exactly how this happens, according to Rogak. "We don't actually train the dogs to jump out of airplanes," Gerry Proctor, former public affairs officer at Lackland said. "That training is done by the [military's] special forces people." The military also hires private contractors to train many of the dogs to parachute, and like special forces personnel, who work in secrecy, they do not generally share training information.

An anonymous member of the Austrian special forces told Rogak that it wasn't as difficult as it might seem to train a dog to parachute because, "Dogs don't perceive height difference [like people do], so that doesn't worry them." He said the roar of the engines bothers the dogs more than the height, and that "once we're on the way down . . . they just enjoy the view."

Handlers wear chest harnesses into which they strap their dog so they can carry the animal against their chests as they parachute together onto land. In some cases, the handler rappels down a line from a helicopter with the dog wearing a vest that is also hooked to the handler. Dogs wear muzzles while parachuting so they won't accidentally bite their tongues or their handlers if they become overexcited or frightened. If parachuting from especially high altitudes, where oxygen levels are low, dogs and handlers wear oxygen masks. If jumping into water, the dog and handler each wear parachutes.

When not learning how to ride on boats or to parachute out of planes, some dogs and their handlers put on demonstrations for the public, usually at military bases or camps around the country. This helps the teams keep in shape. The audience may be preschoolers, veterans, and members of other military units who don't work with dogs. "If we didn't train every day with our dogs, when our dogs go out on missions they would lack the knowledge that they have," says Corporal William Egelston, a dog handler at the Camp Lejeune base in North Carolina. "I think my job is the best in the Marine Corps. I come to work, I play with dogs, I have my own, and he's pretty much my best friend."

TRAINING THE HANDLERS

The Lackland MWD program is also responsible for training some but not all dog handlers and kennel masters. Other handlers may be trained at their home bases. At Lackland, handlers first spend several days in a classroom working with stuffed dogs. They learn about dog behaviors, how to put collars on the animals correctly, how to talk to them, and how to give basic commands such as sit and stay.

Then handlers begin work with big khaki-colored ammunition buckets that stand in for real dogs. Some handlers-in-training even name their buckets! Once more, the handlers practice the basics, such as putting on a dog's collar and leash—this time on the bucket instead of the stuffed animal. They learn how to praise a dog (their bucket) with great enthusiasm. In the "loose dog" exercise, new handlers learn what to do when a MWD (bucket) has escaped its leash. A loose dog could mean trouble for other dogs, so handlers-in-training learn to hold the leash of their own dog tightly and to put the dog's face in their crotch. This position keeps their own dog from seeing the loose dog and reacting aggressively to it.

After a few days, the handlers graduate from working with buckets and are ready to work with real dogs. The winners of a friendly competition get their choice of which dog to work with. These training dogs are experienced dogs that already know the ropes. They are fully qualified but because of illness, injury, or age can no longer serve in a war zone. "The retired dogs at Lackland are your first partner, and they teach you everything you know," said Staff Sergeant Teri Messina, a knowledgeable dog handler at Lackland. "They've served their time."

The handlers practice taking veteran dogs through obstacle courses that include navigating stairs, platforms, and tunnels. The dogs seem to want to help these inexperienced handlers do a good job, says author Maria Goodavage, who has written about MWDs. "C'mon, just follow me, and I'll find the explosive and I'll make you look good, pal," she said about the dogs' attitude. "Collars will inevitably be pulled too tight, commands won't be clear, students will balk or move the wrong way when doing bite training, but the dogs persevere. They're happy to be out of their kennels and working," said Goodavage. Training handlers takes nearly three months, and handlers—not their dogs—must pass a test to prove they can manage their dogs. A graduation ceremony follows, held in a Lackland auditorium. Photographs of handlers who died in action line the walls to remind graduating handlers that they have undertaken a serious and potentially life-threatening job.

DOGS HAVE IT ALL

Dogs naturally have a great sense of smell. But just how good is it? Experts aren't certain. Some say dogs can smell one thousand times better than people or ten thousand times better or even one hundred thousand times better. "Let's suppose they're just 10,000 times better," says Dr. James Walker, former director of the Sensory Research Institute at Florida State University. "If you make the analogy [comparison] to vision, what you and I can see at a third of a mile [0.5 km], a dog could see more than 3,000 miles [4,828 km] away and still see as well [as a human]."

How is this possible? Dog noses are structured very differently than human noses. Dogs have more than 220 million olfactory receptors—nerve cells that detect odors—in their noses. Humans have about 5 million. If you were able to unfold the area in the nose that holds human olfactory receptors, it would be the size of a postage stamp. A bloodhound—the best sniffer of all dogs—would have an area the size of a large handkerchief. When a human inhales, all the air briefly passes over the olfactory receptors and from there goes into the lungs. Humans therefore get only a brief and generalized exposure to odors.

When a dog inhales, much of the air bypasses the receptors and goes

Dogs exhale through the side slits in their noses at the same time they are inhaling oxygen.

straight into the lungs, similar to what happens when a human inhales. However, part of the air a dog inhales goes directly to its scent receptors. Dogs literally collect molecules of odor in the mucous membranes of the receptors, concentrating a very weak smell into an odor that is strong enough to be easily recognized by the animal.

Look carefully at a dog's nose and you'll notice slits on the side of each nostril. While the dog inhales through the nostrils like people do, they can exhale through the slits at the same time they are inhaling. This means that the dog can continue to collect undiluted incoming odors while exhaling used air. Dogs can also move their nostrils independently, which helps them determine from which direction an odor is coming. This is very important when dogs are searching for explosive devices or drugs or when they are tracking a person.

While human brains are ten times bigger than dog brains, the part of the brain that processes odors is proportionally forty times larger in dogs than in people. In addition, dogs have an extra organ—the vomeronasal organ—at the bottom of their nasal cavity. The organ allows dogs to smell and taste at the same time. The vomeronasal organ specializes in detecting pheromones, chemical substances that animals, including dogs, humans, and insects, release naturally. Dogs can therefore discriminate among smells much better than we can. For example, we smell a pizza in the oven. A dog smells the individual odors of the yeast, flour, and oil in pizza dough. It also smells the pepper, basil, oregano, and tomatoes in the sauce, along with the cheese and the spicy odors of sausage, pepperoni, and other toppings.

MWDs use their sight and hearing as well as their sense of smell in their work. Humans and other animals, especially cats and birds, see much better than dogs do. For example, dogs don't see colors as well as we do and they don't see clearly close up. However, dogs have a wider field of vision than humans. When we look straight ahead, we can see about 180 degrees, or half a circle. Much of what humans see is with both eyes (binocular vision) because of where our eyes are positioned on our face. A small part of what we see—our peripheral vision—we see with only one eye (monocular vision). A dog's field of vision is twice as broad, about 250 to 270 degrees, because its eyes are set much farther apart than human eyes. Because dogs' eyes are set on opposite sides of their faces, they have less

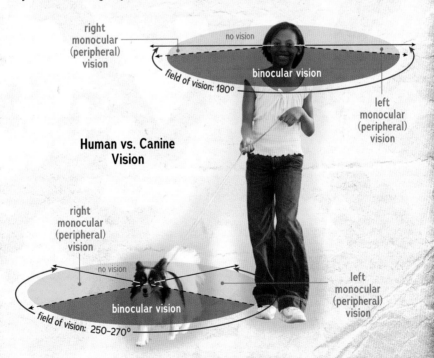

right monocular (peripheral) vision

no vision

binocular vision

field of vision: 180°

left monocular (peripheral) vision

Human vs. Canine Vision

right monocular (peripheral) vision

no vision

binocular vision

field of vision: 250–270°

left monocular (peripheral) vision

binocular vision but have far wider monocular vision than humans. Dogs also see much better in the dark than humans because their eyes have a greater number of light-sensitive cells than we do.

Dogs' ears are sensitive to high-frequency sounds, such as ambulance and police sirens, as well as to sounds that humans can't hear at all. For example, dogs can hear the sound of wind passing over the trip wires that are sometimes used to trigger bombs and booby traps. Humans cannot hear this sound at all. Dogs can hear sounds up to four times farther away than we can. Have you noticed how dogs swivel their ears in different directions when something interests them? These movable ears help dogs locate and focus on specific sounds.

Dogs have it all: a superlative sense of smell, the ability to see better in the dark, and to hear a wider range of sound wave frequencies than humans can. Running at 30 to 45 miles (48 to 72 km) per hour, they are also much faster than people. These traits, combined with dogs' innate desire to please and to play, make them the perfect animal to work with soldiers at peace and at war.

ONE HANDLER'S STORY

Angela Lowe joined the US Air Force in 2006, when she was seventeen. Because she was underage, Angela's mom had to give written permission for her to join the military. Angela says, "It's a funny story. My best friend in high school and I were watching the military channel on television one day after school. We just looked at each other and decided then and there it would be cool to join the Air Force. I had never fired a weapon. I had never owned a dog. I saw a picture of a dog handler on a [recruitment] brochure and decided that was the job I wanted."

Angela worked in the air force security forces for six years before she actually became a dog handler. Only about 10 percent of handlers in the US military are women. "It's a very male dominated career field," Angela says. "I'm the only female in my kennels, and it's kind of intimidating at first to walk into a place with all dominant alpha males [dogs and men]." She has not yet deployed overseas, but that could change at any time.

For the time being, she is stationed at the joint US Air Force/Navy base in Charleston, South Carolina. There, she works with her fourth MWD, Szultan, a young

German shepherd that weighs 75 pounds (34 kg) and has a mind of his own. "I was out in a secluded field with another trainer one day. I wanted to try some off-leash obedience training. As soon as Szultan felt the leash come off, he said, 'See ya lady. I'm outa here.' He took off running through the woods and didn't listen to a word I said. I couldn't even get his attention with a toy. It took twenty minutes to catch him. We were still building rapport and trust at the time."

After a few weeks, the bond between Angela and Szultan grew stronger. "He's a funny dog with a weird personality. We know each other's moods. Some days, he just wakes up on the wrong side of the kennel, so to speak. He'll growl at me one minute, then come up to me and want some love. Now I have a bond with him like no other MWD that I've worked with. He's a quick learner and will do anything I show him. It's an amazing feeling seeing your dog learn new things. I'm his first handler, and that's a pretty cool bond. I've put a lot of work into training Szultan. One of my goals as a handler is to make sure when I pass the leash off to someone else, they have a really great working dog."

US Air Force staff sergeant Angela Lowe, an MWD handler, leads Szultan through an obstacle course in 2014 at the joint US Air Force/Navy base in Charleston, South Carolina. The obstacle course helps prepare the dogs for the challenges they will face when they are deployed.

MYTHS ABOUT MILITARY WORKING DOGS

Mike Dowling, who worked with MWD Rex in Afghanistan, wrote an article for a military website to dispel common myths about MWDs in the media. "To handlers and advocates in the MWD community, it can be frustrating to read and hear about stories that not only are untrue, but are actually harmful [to dogs and handlers]," he said. These myths include the following:

Myth: MWDs bite to kill.

Fact: MWDs are not trained to kill, although they can inflict serious injury. They are trained to apprehend a suspect, which means biting them in a fleshy area of the body and holding on until the handler arrives.

Myth: Any dog can be an MWD, including shelter dogs.

Fact: Only the best dogs of selected breeds, with the appropriate temperament, are suitable for this work. A better use for shelter dogs is to train them as therapy or service dogs for veterans.

Myth: MWDs go home with their handlers after every working day.

Fact: Handlers and their dogs are together 24/7 when on deployment overseas. However, when teams return to their US bases, dogs cannot go home with their handlers at night because they are viewed as valuable military assets. Also, if a potentially dangerous dog were to escape the handler's home and run away or harm someone, the military could face lawsuits. While in the United States, the dogs spend much of their day training or playing with their handlers. They spend nights at their bases in kennels that are clean, safe, and large—about six feet (1.83 meters) wide by twelve feet (3.66 meters) long. After retirement and adoption, however, the dogs spend the rest of their lives in their new owners' homes.

Myth: All MWDs are male.

Fact: Female dogs make great patrol and detection MWDs too.

Myth: MWDs are left behind in war zones or are euthanized.

Fact: While this happened during the Vietnam War, it no longer happens. Because of Robby's Law, 90 percent of retired MWDs are adopted by current or former handlers. Others are adopted by civilians or transferred to police departments. Only dogs that are terminally ill or too aggressive to be retrained for civilian life are euthanized.

CHAPTER 4
PAWS ON THE GROUND

The US military has successfully deployed dogs in war, ever since World War II. Yet the memory of their achievements dims after the conflicts die down and the military reduces funding for dog training programs. Handlers finish their service and leave the military. Dogs are assigned other tasks, given to civilian police departments, or retired and adopted. Mike Dowling says about deploying dogs in the Middle Eastern wars of the twenty-first century, "K9 units hadn't gone to the front line of war since the Vietnam era. As a result we'd lost the know-how to do so. . . . It's our job to learn how to do it all again."

At the height of these Middle Eastern wars, about twenty-five hundred MWDs served with US fighting forces. An estimated 2.5 million Americans have served so far in Afghanistan and Iraq. And when the US military has boots on the ground, paws on the ground are sure to follow.

> "Andy is an amazing dog and he is really great at what he does. Andy to me is more than just a dog. He is my best friend and will always have a special place in my heart. I would do anything for Andy and I know he would do the same for me."
>
> —Specialist Anthony Andrews, handler for Andy, Afghanistan, 2015

US Marine lance corporal Brandon Mann and his MWD, Ty, clear a hill in Sre Kala, Afghanistan, for weapons and IED caches during a patrol in 2012. The United States went to war with Afghanistan shortly after the September 11, 2001, terrorist attacks in the United States.

THE LONGEST WAR

Middle Eastern terrorists hijacked four American airplanes on September 11, 2001. They flew two of the planes into the twin towers of New York's World Trade Center and one into the Pentagon Building in Arlington, Virginia. Passengers stormed the hijackers on the fourth plane—believed to be headed to the White House or the Capitol Building in Washington, DC—forcing it to crash into a Pennsylvania field. Nearly three thousand people died in the 9/11 attacks.

The next month, the United States invaded Afghanistan to overthrow the Taliban, the Islamic fundamentalist political movement ruling the nation at that time. It also targeted al-Qaeda, a global militant Islamist organization founded by Osama bin Laden and based in Afghanistan. US intelligence agencies believed al-Qaeda was responsible for the 9/11 attacks. Two years later, in 2003, the

United States invaded Iraq to topple the government of dictator Saddam Hussein.

The war in Iraq lasted nearly nine years while the war in Afghanistan lasted for almost thirteen years. MWDs had been trained to work in the hot desert and mountain terrains of Iraq and Afghanistan. They had to learn the odors of a dozen or more old and new types of chemical explosives and bomb-making equipment, including dynamite, C4 plastic explosives, ammonium nitrate, potassium chlorate, detonating cord, and smokeless powder. They learned to tolerate the deafening chaos of helicopters, tanks, and combat.

Handler Mike Dowling described a typical mission in Iraq. Mike and his MWD Rex usually spent the day searching for IEDs hidden under mounds of rubble and trash along roads. The enemy had rigged many of the IEDs of that period so they could trigger them with a simple cell phone call. Bomb makers would connect electrical wire to a cell phone's antenna and from there to a car battery and then to the hidden IEDs. The bomb maker could then watch through binoculars from a distance. When US soldiers, war dogs, or other military personnel neared a hidden IED, the bomb maker used a second cell phone to call the rigged cell phone. When that cell phone rang, it completed an electrical circuit and set off the bomb. Other IEDs were set to explode when someone stepped on a pressure plate hidden under the sand.

THE US MILITARY ESTIMATES THAT IEDS CAUSED BETWEEN ONE-HALF AND TWO-THIRDS OF US DEATHS AND INJURIES IN IRAQ AND AFGHANISTAN.

Enemy combatants in the Middle East typically placed IEDs in towns and villages or along roads, hiding them in vehicles and deserted houses. Suicide bombers would wear IEDs in suicide vests, head for a crowded area, and then trigger the device to explode. Often exploding IEDs signaled the beginning of a battle, with gunfire and more IED explosions to follow. The US military estimates that IEDs caused between one-half and two-thirds of US deaths and injuries in Iraq and Afghanistan. As of summer 2016, the US death toll in both countries had neared seven thousand, while at least nine hundred thousand had been injured.

OUTSIDE THE WIRE

MWDs deployed to Afghanistan performed several important tasks. About 95 percent of the dogs' work in Afghanistan was sniffing out bombs. They also searched cars and trucks, deserted mud huts, rocky roadsides, and fields filled with crops of grapes and grain for hidden enemy insurgents. Dogs protected their handlers, patrolled and guarded American bases, and saved American lives.

Dog teams routinely go outside the wire—leaving the safety of the base—to conduct missions. For example, in *Glory Hounds*, a 2013 Animal Planet documentary about four dog teams in Afghanistan, viewers follow handlers and dogs as they enter private homes where Taliban insurgents often hid weapons and bomb-making materials among civilian families. Dog teams were responsible for clearing an area—ensuring it was safe—before other soldiers entered. "Our goal is to . . . save someone's life, especially American lives," US Marine Kent Ferrell said of his work with MWD Zora. "That's what we're [in Afghanistan] for. That's our job."

Just how good are MWDs at saving lives? Technical Sergeant Justin Kitts received a Bronze Star (a US military decoration awarded for heroic or meritorious achievement in combat) in 2011 for his work in Afghanistan with his dog Dyngo. The US military credits Kitts and Dyngo with having protected civilians and thirty thousand US and coalition forces (units from other nations that fought alongside US military personnel) during the pair's sixty-three missions outside the wire. During those operations, Dyngo discovered 370 pounds (167 kg) of explosive materials and several IEDs. "You automatically [go on dangerous missions] because of the training you've had as a team to respond to different events," Kitts said. "For me, I felt comfortable being outside the wire. I knew it was my job, and I went out and did it."

Brandon Liebert, who deployed overseas with his dog Monty, described a particularly productive day when they searched an abandoned house. In one room, they found an antiaircraft gun and then "Monty found over six hundred antiaircraft rounds. . . . I was so proud of him, and he was really happy, because he knew he did a great job." That impressive find potentially saved the lives of dozens of people. Before the US military deployed MWDs to Iraq and Afghanistan, soldiers were able to detect only about half of the IEDs believed to be hidden in war zones before they exploded. After dogs joined the soldiers, the detection rate increased to 80 percent.

Usually, dogs protect their handlers, but sometimes it happens the other way around. US Marine sergeant Mark Vierig described an incident that occurred when he and his MWD, Lex, were deployed in Afghanistan. The team was protecting a platoon of construction workers who were paving a long road. As the men finished one section of road, they moved to the next section, digging protective foxholes to sleep in at night. One night, as Vierig worked to dig a foxhole big enough for him and Lex, Taliban fighters fired an explosive round that went off 30 feet (9 m) from Lex, who was crouching beside Vierig. Vierig grabbed Lex by the scruff of his neck and slung him into the shallow foxhole, then lay over the dog's body to protect him. The next shell exploded 15 feet (4.6 m) away. Vierig's body armor and Kevlar (bulletproof vest) protected the two of them. Lex remained calm. "When stuff goes down in a situation like that, dogs know what's going on," he said. "They're like, 'OK, this is serious.'" As Vierig says, "[facing danger] is a lot better when you're with your dog."

SEND A CANINE CARE PACKAGE

You and your friends or classmates can do something special for a dog serving overseas by collecting money for a canine care package and sending it to the United States War Dogs Association. Military working dogs need items such as K9 booties, doggles, large rope and Kong chew toys, grooming tools, flea and tick medications, K9 toothbrushes and toothpaste, collapsible nylon bowls for food and water, chewy treats, shampoo and conditioner, nail clippers, and cooling vests and mats to use in hot desert environments. These supplies cost money, and your collection can help. In fact, you can specify what items you'd like the association to include in your canine care package. The association will purchase the products and send them in your name or your school's name to a handler and dog in need. For more information, visit http://www.uswardogs.org/k9-care/.

BONDING AGAIN

When dog handlers finish their tours of duty, dogs that are still in good health and young enough to continue the rigorous life of a MWD are assigned to new handlers. But the bond between dog and handler is so intense, so close, that people may wonder how a dog makes the transition to a new handler. That can be tricky, according to Burnam. "Trainers and dogs are bonded in a loving partnership built over time together on and off the battlefield," he says. "They look after one another wherever they are. However, it's not always a smooth transition for a dog or handler to go from one partner to another. It takes time and training to make the change. Some dogs take longer than others and some never really get over a particular partner." Dogs that cannot adapt to new handlers can no longer serve as MWDs and are put up for adoption.

US Air Force staff sergeant Brent Olson knows how difficult the transition can be. He had less than three months to build a relationship with MWD Blek. He was paired with him after officials assigned the dog's previous handler to other duties. Blek had worked with several handlers and was more adaptable than many dogs. To build trust, Olson frequently visited Blek in his kennel to brush, groom, and pet the dog. Olson also played with Blek often, letting him off the leash to chase a ball. Dogs come to trust the person who feeds them and grooms them and plays with them. Blek was especially outgoing and willing to work as long as he got plenty of play and praise.

Staff Sergeant Karl Stefanowicz, who worked with several MWDs before adopting his former partner Maci in 2014, feels it's extremely important to make a good transition. "There will be a down time where the dog is no longer worked. He just sort of hangs out. When the new handler is ready to start, they go through what is called the rapport process to help build the bond between handler and dog. The handler takes the dog for walks, brushes the dog and plays with him to say, 'Hey, I'm your new dad.' Each kennel has different approaches to how it should be done." When Karl was newly partnered with Maci, "I would always feed him and stay with him until he was finished eating. I would also give him some treats throughout the day to let him know that I was there."

DRESSED FOR THE JOB

Soldiers aren't the only ones who wear uniforms on duty. MWDs may wear doggles (goggles for dogs) to protect their eyes from blowing sand, debris, and the harsh sunlight of desert environments. They can wear booties to protect their paws from rocks, sand, cracked pavement, and other surfaces dangerous to their paws. Most dogs wear collars, leashes, halters, and even bulletproof Kevlar vests.

Parachuting vests allow dogs and handlers to jump in tandem or separately. Handlers can provide hearing protection for their dogs—doggie earmuffs—when the animals are in a noisy environment they aren't used to, such as on a helicopter or under unexpected gunfire. Some dogs that work off the leash also wear a global positioning system (GPS) device so their handlers can easily track and locate them if they venture too far.

An American MWD in Parwan Province, Afghanistan, wears doggles to protect his eyes as a helicopter takes off, kicking up dust and debris.

CAIRO IN PAKISTAN

"There was a dog?" President Barack Obama asked as the commander of the US Navy's SEAL Team 6 described the mission in Pakistan that had killed Osama bin Laden, perhaps the most wanted terrorist on the planet. "I want to meet that dog." Cairo, a handsome Belgian Malinois, waited in the next room, muzzled at the request of the president's Secret Service team. "If you want to meet the dog, Mr. President, I advise you to bring treats," the SEAL commander joked. The president first congratulated the commander. Then Cairo's handler brought in the muzzled dog to meet the president, who bent over and stroked him.

In a daring nighttime raid on May 2, 2011, US Navy SEALs stormed the urban compound in Abbottabad, Pakistan, where bin Laden and his family had been living for years, and killed him. Cairo was the only mission member of Team 6 that was publicly identified. To protect the confidentiality of this special ops mission and to ensure the safety of participants, the US Navy did not release the names of SEAL Team 6 members.

Only about 1 percent of MWDs qualify as SEAL dogs. Cairo had the skills expected of a special ops soldier. He was trained to shimmy down ropes while tied to his handler and to parachute from planes over water. He could detect explosives and could locate and hold people as well. Six SEALS entered the compound to search for bin Laden. Meanwhile, Cairo, four SEALs, and an American translator of Pakistani origin who spoke Urdu, patrolled the compound perimeter to keep curious neighbors away. If the SEALs couldn't find bin Laden inside, they planned to send in Cairo to search for false walls or hidden doors behind which bin Laden might have been hiding. The team successfully located bin Laden, shot him, and buried him at sea, after holding a traditional Islamic funeral. Cairo and the SEALs completed their mission without injury to themselves.

The dog involved in the US Navy SEAL operation that killed terrorist Osama bin Laden was a Belgian Malinois, like this MWD—Bodro—training with his handler (US Air Force staff sergeant Patrick D. Spivey) at a US airfield in Afghanistan.

MWDs such as Cairo that work with the US Navy's Sea, Air, and Land teams and other special operations (special ops) units, wear as much specialized equipment as their human counterparts. On the SEALs' mission in Pakistan to capture Osama bin Laden in 2011, for example, Cairo wore a K9 storm intruder vest (a superstrong, flexible body armor) like the vests that human SEALs with him wore. Cairo also wore doggles fitted with night vision and infrared lenses to allow him to see human heat forms through concrete walls. Cairo wore a remotely operated video camera and antenna on his back so his handlers could see from his vantage point.

On some special ops missions, dogs also wear audio recorders, earbuds, or a microphone. This allows handlers, who may be at some distance from their dogs, to see and hear what the dogs see and hear. Handlers can give commands to their dogs through a microphone, based on what they observe on the dog's camera. For example, handlers may want to call the dogs back without giving away their position to the enemy. These battery-powered canine tactical assault suits may cost up to $86,000 each.

FIRST AID IN THE FIELD

Military working dogs get some of the best veterinary care in the world to keep them in top condition. "Our primary mission is to provide medical care for the military working dogs," Captain Allison Brekke, veterinarian at Moody Air Force Base in Valdosta, Georgia, said. "We maintain their preventive care through vaccinations, parasite control, and general wellness screenings to keep them fit to fight. We also run a vet clinic on base [for animals in the local community] as a means to keep up our medical skills, so we can continue to provide care to the working dogs."

Being a MWD is difficult and sometimes dangerous. Dogs get hurt, no matter how closely their handlers watch out for them. So Emily Pieracci, former US Army Veterinary Corps Officer at Arizona's Yuma Proving Ground, designed educational programs to train handlers at Yuma to deal with animal injuries once they are deployed overseas. While at Yuma, her job was to care for the dogs during training and to teach handlers how to keep their dogs alive if they were to be injured. While veterinarians typically see MWDs once a month when they and their handlers are in the United States, it may be up to the handlers to provide both routine and emergency care in a war zone.

"Handlers are the first responders if their dog gets hurt," Pieracci says. "I focused on treatments that dogs may need while deployed, such as placing IV [intravenous] catheters on plastic dummy dogs, bandaging techniques for potential IED injuries, giving injections of medication, splinting [stabilizing] broken bones, and cleaning ears and eyes. The courses I taught covered everything from cutting toenails to performing CPR [cardiopulmonary resuscitation to trigger breathing and heartbeat]." Just as nursing and medical students practice CPR and other procedures on human manikins, handlers practice on dog manikins that come complete with an artificial pulse and lungs.

Pieracci's three-day course included reacting to surprise injuries. "For example, the handler may clear a building, and I'd announce that an IED hit the dog.

A US Marine handler comforts his MWD after the canine was injured and rescued by a helicopter in southern Afghanistan in 2011.

The handler would have to call for a Medevac [evacuation by military helicopter] while placing an IV and bandaging the dog. We incorporated medical emergencies during night training so handlers learned how night vision goggles affected handlers' depth perception while giving first aid to the dogs."

Training at Yuma occurs in a desert environment similar to that of Iraq and Afghanistan. "I saw injuries many other vets didn't see," Pieracci says. "I treated snake bites and scorpion stings, for example. Dogs are curious creatures and they love to explore new terrain. They'll stick their nose down in a burrow in the sand, and the next thing you know, 'Wham!' they've been bit or stung."

Other common medical challenges include heat-related injuries. "The dogs are subject to heat stroke because the summer temperature [at Yuma and in the Middle East] can exceed 105°F (41°C). The dogs have trouble walking and responding to commands when they have heat stroke; they act like they're intoxicated," Pieracci says. Handlers are taught to take their dogs' temperature every two hours while working in such hot weather. The dogs must be cooled down if their temperature exceeds 102°F (39°C). "Handlers are trained to recognize the signs of heat stress in their dogs and instructed to stop working the dog before reaching that critical point. Lots of water, shade, and IV fluids are needed to help over-heated dogs," Pieracci says.

Sometimes MWDs don't like to travel, or they feel uncomfortable in unfamiliar places. "MWDs get emotionally and mentally stressed in new environments and during deployments, just like people do," Pieracci says. "Upset stomach, nausea, and diarrhea are common ailments we

> "I SAW INJURIES MANY OTHER VETS DIDN'T SEE. I TREATED SNAKE BITES AND SCORPION STINGS, FOR EXAMPLE. DOGS ARE CURIOUS CREATURES AND THEY LOVE TO EXPLORE NEW TERRAIN.... AND THE NEXT THING YOU KNOW, 'WHAM!' THEY'VE BEEN BIT OR STUNG."
>
> —EMILY PIERACCI

treat MWDs for. These symptoms usually resolve in a couple days with a mixture of TLC from their handlers, a reduced training schedule, and a bland diet to settle their stomachs." The US military evacuates badly injured dogs serving in overseas war zones to military veterinary centers that might be hundreds of miles away or even farther in Germany and the United States. There the dogs get treatment and rehabilitation.

POTUS AND THE POPE

Military working dogs and their handlers do a lot of their work in the United States. Not only do the teams serve at nearly every military base in the country, but they also guard the president of the United States, or POTUS, and official governmental visitors such as foreign leaders and Pope Francis, the leader of the Roman Catholic Church. The dogs frequently go on temporary duty, or TDY. "I've been on TDYs with the Secret Service," MWD handler Angela Lowe says. "They've included New York City, Green Bay, Wisconsin, and Charlotte, North Carolina, among others. All of these missions were for POTUS and other dignitaries."

The Secret Service—the agency charged with protecting the president and vice president of the United States—has its own dog teams. However, the agency often borrows teams from the military for specific domestic missions, including patrols and searches for explosives. Dog handler Karl Stefanowicz and his dog Maci went to New Orleans, Louisiana, in 2013 for a presidential visit. "We did route clearance for where President Obama's motorcade was going through, then we were on emergency hold a few blocks away." US Marine Corps dog handler Bret Reynolds and his dog Bernie also guarded President Obama in Los Angeles as well as visiting former president Asif Ali Zardari of Pakistan in Washington, DC. Dog teams guard other officials as well, such as members of the president's cabinet and US Supreme Court justices. Local police departments also can request MWD teams if they need more dogs for patrolling large gatherings and special events.

When Pope Francis visited the United States in the fall of 2015, dog teams helped to ensure his safety at every stop. For example, when he visited Philadelphia, Pennsylvania, Staff Sergeant Marshall Rains and MWD Rea, along

Bret Reynolds, a MWD handler with the US Marine Corps, and his working dog Bernie have guarded political officials in the United States, including US president Barack Obama.

with Staff Sergeant Lance Brennan and MWD Akim, all from Oklahoma's Vance Air Force Base, joined the security team assigned to protect the pope. Before the pope arrived in Philadelphia, the teams swept the areas he would be visiting for bombs and explosives. After Pope Francis arrived, the teams worked at checkpoints, inspecting and questioning people who entered secure areas where large crowds were gathered to see the pope.

The teams took separate commercial flights from Oklahoma to Atlanta, Georgia, and from there to Philadelphia. The dogs rode in the passenger cabin with their handlers. "My pup slept on all four flights [there and back]," Brennan said of Akim. "He was nervous while we were at the terminal and once we started to taxi he wanted to go on the floor and he just slept. Normally [Akim] is kind of jittery and antsy. . . . The entire time we were [in Philadelphia] he was just calm, cool and collected. It was actually really nice." As specially trained security dogs, Akim and Rea were allowed to stay in the hotel room with their handlers instead of sleeping in their kennels.

67

Dogs on Deployment

MWDs aren't the only dogs involved in military life. How about the young man who wants to join the US Army? What happens to his collie while he's gone? Or the single mom with a young child who joins the US Marines? What happens to her golden retriever and the child? Maybe her sister can take the child but is allergic to dogs. What then? Finding care for a beloved pet during military service may make the difference between joining the military or not.

The nonprofit organization Dogs on Deployment helps military members find temporary homes for their companion animals. Dogs on Deployment says it provides a "central network for military members to find volunteers willing to board their pets while they are deployed or have other service commitments, making them unable to temporarily care for their pets. No pet should ever be surrendered to a shelter due to a military commitment."

Since 2011 Dogs on Deployment has found foster homes for more than eight hundred animals whose military owners were deployed or could not take care of their pets for a period of time. The organization is an online networking service. It does not directly arrange for boarding services. Service members needing temporary care for their animals must first register with the organization. Once approved, the service member can search the site for a foster home that meets the animal's needs. Service members and foster parents (who also must be registered with and approved by Dogs on Deployment as animal caregivers) arrange a meet and greet to be sure the animal fits into the potential foster home.

The organization's Facebook page posts information about the program along with photos and details about animals needing a temporary home. For example, a Facebook exchange from November 1, 2015, said, "Military member in North Carolina needs help from a [Dogs on Deployment boarder] to watch his dog Argos. Argos is a very happy dog who loves to run outside and play fetch. He is completely housebroken and very polite inside. He is good with cats and other dogs. Can you help?" Within twenty-four hours, Argos had a new foster mom who wrote, "His owner and I connected on the website and Argos is with me!"

TOP DOGS

Greg Madrid and his MWD Pablo normally work at the Marine Corps Logistics Base in Albany, Georgia, and are often sent on TDYs within the state. Madrid and Pablo have protected presidents Barack Obama and Bill Clinton as well as Vice President Joseph Biden. Pablo also regularly attends Sunday services at a church in Plains, Georgia, where he helps protect former president Jimmy Carter while he teaches Bible study classes. Greg and Pablo also participate in school career days and in charity events in the region to show people how dogs and handlers work together. Pablo is such an exceptional dog that the American Kennel Association

In London on April 5, 2016, gunnery sergeant Christopher Willingham, of Tuscaloosa, Alabama, shakes hands with retired MWD Lucca, after the dog received the PDSA (People's Dispensary for Sick Animals) Dickin Medal for animal bravery. The twelve-year-old German shepherd lost her leg in 2012 in Afghanistan when she was searching for IEDs. When a device detonated, she instantly lost her front left leg. The award is the highest any animal can receive while serving in military conflict.

named him dog of the year in the canine excellence uniform division in 2015. "I've had [Pablo] for three years and he's just a great working dog, great companion, very sociable," Madrid says of the 80-pound (36 kg) Belgian Malinois. "He's a very big teddy bear, but he does know how to turn it on whenever it is time to go to work."

MWD Lucca made history in April 2016 when she became the first American dog to receive the United Kingdom's Dickin Medal, considered the highest military honor for animals worldwide. When deployed to Afghanistan in 2012 with her handler Juan Rodriguez—a member of the US Army Special Forces—Lucca lost her left front leg when she stepped on a bomb that blasted her into the air. She received treatment from army veterinarians in Kandahar Province, and within ten days of her injury, she had learned to walk on three legs. At the award ceremony at Wellington Barracks near Buckingham Palace in London, England, Jan McLoughlin, director general of the PDSA organization awarding the medal, said, "Lucca's conspicuous gallantry and devotion to duty makes her a hugely deserving recipient of . . . the Dickin Medal. Her ability and determination to seek out arms and explosives preserved human life amid some of the world's fiercest military conflicts."

CHAPTER 5
COMING HOME

Most Americans believe that four-footed veterans have as much right to a happy retirement as two-legged veterans. Under US law, the military is obligated to do everything it can to find adoptive homes for dogs that have completed their military working lives. The DoD has a cradle-to-grave philosophy for its dogs and says that none are left behind. "These dogs are treated like Marines," says Bill Childress, program manager for the US Marine Corps military working dog program. "We bring everybody home."

Even with the best veterinary care in the world, MWDs sooner or later must retire. In some cases, they have completed their military service or can no longer work because of injury. Some dogs simply lose their enthusiasm for the job. After retiring from military

"Bernie was one of a kind, very bubbly and outgoing. She transitioned from the hard life of being a military working dog to living on my couch. Bernie's gone now, but she had four happy years of retirement hanging out with my other dogs. She was up there in age, and with three combat tours in Iraq, she had done her time."

— Bret Reynolds, former US Marines sergeant and handler for Bernie, 2015

A police officer and his dog, Buster, watch pedestrians in the subway station in Times Square in New York City after a car bomb was discovered in the area in 2010 before it detonated. After retirement from life as an MWD, many dogs work for law enforcement agencies.

service, a dog in good health may be offered to a civilian law enforcement agency to work another couple of years in a local police department or sheriff's office. Some serve as training dogs to help new handlers learn the job. But most dogs find happy homes with current or former handlers. In fact, handlers adopt about 90 percent of retiring MWDs. Lackland manages the adoption of all military working dogs based in the United States and has placed thousands of retired MWDs in private homes since 2000.

READY TO RETIRE

An information page on the United States War Dogs Association website says about retiring MWDs, "Please remember that no matter what their type, sex, or color, these retired military dogs were selected by the Department of Defense for their stable and outgoing temperaments. They make wonderful companions, and they deserve great homes."

The traits that make a MWD good at its job are the same traits that make a dog a good companion animal. According to Stewart Hilliard, who heads Lackland's breeding program, the adoption process really starts in puppyhood when potential MWDs are first selected. "We choose the dogs for sociability, good character, and friendliness, in addition to drive and bravery," he said. "An astonishing number of these dogs make nice pets because we select for those traits from the beginning. We have adopted out scores and scores of MWDs with very little in the way of difficulties. They do best with adoptive families who keep their obedience training up, give them limits and controls, and treat them like the strong and 'worthy of respect' animals they are."

The adoption process for a retiring MWD begins when the dog's kennel master, animal behaviorists, and veterinarians evaluate the dog to be sure it is healthy and good-natured enough to become a companion animal in someone's home. MWDs have been trained to attack on command. To provide a safe environment for adoptive parents and for the dog, experts test the dogs to be sure they don't display unacceptable aggression toward people or other animals. The dogs' innate good nature ensures that most of them are good candidates for adoption. Most would never attack a person unless ordered to do so or to protect their handlers and families, much like any dog would do. Dogs waiting for their new homes live in the kennels at Lackland, where trainers and volunteers play with the dogs every day. It doesn't take long for the dogs to mellow out.

THE TRAITS THAT MAKE A MWD GOOD AT ITS JOB ARE THE SAME TRAITS THAT MAKE A DOG A GOOD COMPANION ANIMAL.

Bret Reynolds, who adopted his MWD Bernie, describes part of the assessment each retiring dog goes through. "Dr. Emily Pieracci was the vet [who assessed Bernie]. She checked out Bernie's medical and dental health. Bernie's hips were weak, and Dr. Pieracci decided it was time she retired." Then Bernie went through some tests. "We took a videotape of Bernie to Lackland to determine if her temperament was good enough to be adopted. The tape showed how Bernie responded to everyday situations. While she was on leash, people dressed in street clothes walked by her, stopped and talked with one another, argued with each other, and ran away, while observers watched in the background," Bret said." A dog must not show aggression toward the people arguing or act as if it wants to chase the person who is running. Also, dogs cannot react when someone takes away their food or toy. Bernie remained calm and relaxed in each situation.

The adoption coordinator then reviews the list of people waiting for a retired MWD. Often the dog's current and previous handlers express interest in adopting their wartime buddy. Lackland also considers families of dog handlers killed in action. That process may take a few weeks to several months. While members of the public can apply to adopt a retired MWD, they may have to wait a year or more to receive a dog because handlers and military families have first priority.

Prospective adoptive parents fill out an application with basic information. Are there other animals or children in the house? A fenced yard? What are the prospective adoptive parents looking for in a retired MWD—a guard dog or a companion animal? An active dog or one that is more laid-back? Available dogs may include Belgian Malinois, German shepherds, Dutch shepherds, Labrador retrievers, and occasionally mixed breeds.

Applicants who pass the application process then meet with adoption coordinators and visit one or more dogs at Lackland. Once the parents select a dog suited to their interests and home life, the adoption coordinator sends the dog to the veterinarian for a final checkup. If approved, the dog can be released to its new owners. While the adoption is free, the new parents are responsible for the costs of transporting the dog from Lackland to their home, wherever that may be, and for all future veterinary care. Adopted dogs may end up in any state, depending on where their former handlers or new adoptive parents live.

The new parents also must sign a contract transferring ownership of the dog from the DoD to themselves. The new owners must agree the dog will not be used for illegal purposes, police activity, or for any business activities that involve profit. The dog is to be a companion animal only. And finally, the new owners must release the DoD from legal responsibility for the dog. For example, if a retired MWD bites another animal or a person, the owner cannot hold the DoD responsible for injuries. After the paperwork is done and the dog has passed its medical checkup, dog and adoptive parents head off to make a new home together.

HOME SWEET HOME

Since the early 2000s, the average age of retiring MWDs has dropped from ten years to eight and a half years, largely because their job has gotten tougher. Before the Iraq and Afghanistan conflicts, most MWDs guarded American bases around the world. Since then MWDs have been deployed to hot desert environments and high mountain passes, where they jump over fences and deep trenches, cross rickety bridges, climb steep stairs, and run over extremely rocky and mountainous terrain. MWDs work hard. They are true athletes!

Meet Maci, Robbie, Iva, and Ikar, four war dogs that completed their service and are enjoying their well-earned retirement, happy and secure with their former handlers and their families.

KARL STEFANOWICZ AND MACI

"Maci is a 73-pound [33 kg] black German shepherd who thinks he's a lap dog," says Staff Sergeant Karl Stefanowicz of Columbus Air Force Base near Columbus, Mississippi. "All he wants to do is run around and play. I call him a wrecking ball because he has no sense of how big he actually is. He's always been more of a lover than a fighter. The whole time I worked with Maci in patrol work—where his assignment was to attack and hold—you could tell he'd be like, 'If I have to I will, but I'd rather give kisses.' His good nature doesn't stop him from protecting me and my family, though. He growled at someone who came to my door recently. It was the first time in three years that I'd heard him growl!"

Maci worked in Afghanistan as an explosive-detection dog with another handler before he became Karl's partner in February 2013. "Maci is a true war hero and has saved many lives," Karl says. He and Maci served on a US Air Force base in the Middle Eastern nation of Oman for six months until Maci's hip problems became serious enough that Karl pushed for him to come home early. The team returned to Columbus Air Force Base. There, the pair worked as a patrol team to prevent intruders from slipping onto the base. Occasionally, they would leave the base to protect VIPs, including President Obama, or to give demonstrations for the public.

Eventually, a veterinarian determined that Maci's hip problems were so severe that he could no longer serve in the military at all. The military officially retired Maci in October 2014. How did he fit into his new life? "Maci is just another family member," Karl says. "He has his own special bed and relaxes with the rest of us. We have a four-month-old son and two cats. Maci is very protective of my son. He lies down next to him and watches over him, and you can see he has that bond with the baby already. He ignores the cats and they don't really enjoy him being around, but they deal with it! Maci learned quickly where he was in the pack and that he needed to protect my family like he did me." Karl adds, "While we are deployed and away from home and family, these dogs are our family. They keep us sane. They are the real heroes and our best friends."

> "THESE DOGS ARE OUR FAMILY. THEY KEEP US SANE. THEY ARE THE REAL HEROES AND OUR BEST FRIENDS."
>
> —KARL STEFANOWICZ

CHARLIE HARDESTY AND ROBBIE

"Robbie is an amazing animal who has been a blessing to my family and me," says US Marine staff sergeant Charles D. Hardesty, Kennel Master at Marine Corps Air Ground Combat Center in Twentynine Palms, California, about his adopted Belgian Malinois. "He's a giant teddy bear who loves everyone he meets. As soon as you offer your hand to pet him, you're his friend. He judges no one and is there for you through thick and thin. When we were first partnered, Robbie was an anxious dog. Belgian Malinois are very excitable and have a high drive, but Robbie seemed to be one step closer to crazy. We bonded fairly well and training went well for us. We then went through an eight-week course to become a Combat Tracking Dog Team."

The marines deployed Charlie and Robbie to Afghanistan in 2009. "We were there to help locate and contact the enemy, and to find lost personnel. For the majority of the time we worked on a joint task force with a British parachute regiment." One day, an IED blast knocked Charlie to the ground. He came to a few moments later to find a fierce firefight in progress. Robbie was still by his side. He looked at Charlie with his round, fearful eyes as if to say, "What the [heck] just happened?" Charlie helped an injured soldier and then returned to be sure Robbie was safe. The dog kept right on braving the sound of bullets, even though the blast and gunfire clearly frightened him.

When Charlie and Robbie returned to the United States in 2010, the military sent them to Yuma Proving Ground. "That's where Robbie and I parted ways. He was assigned to another handler and deployed again." Charlie and Robbie were reunited in 2012 when Charlie adopted him. "Robbie has definitely transitioned very well since his adoption. He gets along great with both my small children. We have another dog and they also get along well. Robbie is definitely retired, as his current personality is very laid-back. He doesn't get too excited about anything these days." Charlie adds, "Robbie and I had the opportunity to go on the *Conan* [late-night] show. That was an amazing opportunity that I would never have had if I hadn't met Robbie."

DUSTIN WEEKS AND IVA

"Iva has a great personality," says Technical Sergeant Dustin Weeks, stationed at Columbus Air Force Base. "She is a very vocal dog and affectionate. She loves to be petted and will bring a toy and put it in your lap to get attention." Dustin and Iva—an all-black German shepherd—were paired in 2013. Iva had been previously deployed with other handlers to Afghanistan and to a US air base in the United Arab Emirates.

After Dustin and Iva teamed up, they returned to Afghanistan. "Our most important task was explosive detection. We were selected to be part of an Army Special Forces team and our main job was to clear roadways and villages—to look for IEDs and weapons caches. There were also a few times where our camp came under rocket attacks and sometimes the enemy's rockets didn't explode when they hit the ground. Iva and I would locate the impact site of the rocket, and our Explosive Ordinance Disposal unit would detonate the unexploded rocket."

Dustin and Iva also served a tour of duty in the Middle Eastern nation of Qatar. "When the military deploys an MWD to a location that is not a war zone [such as Qatar and the United Arab Emirates], the team conducts searches at the commercial vehicle inspection area and conducts mobile patrols throughout the base. The biggest advantage of having a MWD is the psychological

Dustin Weeks adopted his MWD, Iva *(right)*, in 2015 after serving with her in Afghanistan.

deterrent capability," Dustin says. In other words, few people are likely to argue with a soldier accompanied by a well-trained war dog!

Dustin adopted Iva in 2015, and she fits well into his family. "I have two dachshunds at home and she gets along just fine with them," he says. "I also have a young daughter who loves to play with her. Iva has full access to my house and I have a doggy door that leads into a fenced-in back yard."

Dustin is proud of the work Iva has done. "She has been a true asset to the United States Air Force. Along with her four overseas deployments, she also accompanied the United States Secret Service on multiple occasions across the globe to provide explosive detection support for the entire cabinet [presidential advisory team] of the White House, including the president and vice president. In addition, Iva has also been utilized throughout the Columbus community and the state to search for explosives during numerous bomb threats."

VANCE MCFARLAND AND IKAR

"I am so grateful he was found alive and is well," Army Specialist Vance McFarland said when he learned that he could adopt his former partner, Czech shepherd Ikar. "I am even more thankful that I get the opportunity to give Ikar the proper home, love, and attention he deserves from this point on. He will live out the rest of his life being treated like the hero he is." While Vance was in the US military, Ikar was a contract working dog owned and trained by an Indiana kennel. In other words, the US Army paid the kennel to train some of their soldiers and to hire their dogs. Ikar was just over one year old when he and Vance completed their training in IED detection at the Indiana kennel and deployed to Afghanistan.

"The bond and amount of trust we had in each other was stronger than anything I could ever explain to another person," Vance said. "We had a dangerous mission and we needed each other to do our jobs, not just to save ourselves, but to bring our fellow paratroopers [parachutists] home alive and in one piece. On our very first combat patrol outside the wire in Afghanistan we found our first IED."

Ikar, a sniffer dog, rides with handler Vance McFarland, a specialist in the US Army's 82nd Airborne Division, in May 2012. Their team is in an armored vehicle outside Forward Operating Base (FOB) Pasab in Kandahar Province in southern Afghanistan.

COMING HOME

Vance and Ikar returned to the United States after their deployment ended in 2012. But within minutes of walking off the plane at Fort Bragg, North Carolina, the contractors who owned Ikar took him away to serve another tour of duty in Afghanistan with a new handler. Vance went on to his assigned duties but never stopped thinking about Ikar. "I would always look back on the memories I have of us and the nights we spent together sleeping on the dirt at some outpost or in some shady abandoned Afghan compound in the middle of Taliban land. Everyone would be scattered around on the dirt floor or in cots, while I'm sitting there huddled up with my four-legged partner thinking what an awesome job I have and how lucky I was to hang out and work with a dog all day."

Vance didn't know that the contract company had temporarily placed Ikar and nearly a dozen other bomb-sniffing dogs in a kennel in Virginia in 2014. The company thought it would soon have more work for the dogs. The kennel owner, at great personal expense, cared for the dogs, exercised them, and loved them while waiting seventeen months for the contractor to find new work for the dogs or to reclaim them. But that never happened. The kennel owner turned the dogs over to Mission K9 Rescue and the US War Dogs Association so those organizations could attempt to locate the dogs' former handlers and reunite them.

Mission K9 Rescue posted pictures of the dogs on Facebook, and soon Vance and Ikar were reunited at the Boise, Idaho, airport. Would the five-year-old Ikar recognize Vance after three years? TV stations and newspapers waited at the airport to find out. Vance, fidgeting in the arrival area and holding a big red Kong toy, called to Ikar as a Mission K9 Rescue volunteer walked the dog off the plane. Ikar raced into Vance's arms. "He is going to live the rest of his retired life spoiled. Really spoiled," Vance said. "I will forever be in debt to all the people who made this reunion possible. I could not say thank you enough times for you all to know how much this means to me!"

MORE WAR DOGS COME HOME

Most MWDs and their handlers share the same home base in the United States—at least while they are partnered. Some dogs, however, have a permanent home base in another country, such as Japan, South Korea, Germany, or Qatar. While

MWD Journalist Adopts Dyngo

Rebecca Frankel has written about war dogs since 2010 for the international *Foreign Policy* magazine and has been a television news commentator as well. She researched and wrote the book *War Dogs: Tales of Canine Heroism, History, and Love.* While doing so, she met and interviewed many MWD handlers and got to know their dogs.

She first met MWD Dyngo and his then handler Justin Kitts at Lackland Air Force Base in 2012. "While I was reporting I tried my best to not have favorite dogs. But I found that's nearly impossible; animals are like people, they have their own individual personalities and it makes sense (to my mind) that certain people get on with certain dogs more than others. And it's no exaggeration to say that I dug Dyngo right from the get-go."

In December 2015, Dyngo's new handler Sergeant Nofo Lilo, sent her a note saying, "Hey Rebecca, would you like to adopt Dyngo?" Neither Kitts nor Lilo could adopt Dyngo. Rebecca had connected with Kitts, Lilo, and Dyngo several times, and they both thought of her when it came time for the eleven-year-old Belgian Malinois to retire after multiple tours in Afghanistan.

Rebecca had to go through the same process as other prospective adoptive parents. In May 2016 in an article for *Foreign Policy*, she wrote about her happy news, "I'll be traveling to Luke Air Force Base in Phoenix, Arizona, to pick up [Dyngo]. What better way could there be to come full circle on six and a half years of writing about war dogs?"

deployed, they are part of the US military. The handlers come and go, while the dogs remain attached to the base. At retirement, the dogs can be adopted by a current or former handler or by another service member who lives in that country.

Sometimes American handlers living overseas may decide to return to the United States, hoping to bring their MWDs with them. In the past, retired foreign-based MWDs were not considered part of the US military and could not be flown back to the US at military expense. If a former handler (or another adoptive family in the United States) wanted to adopt the dog, the handler or other adoptive parent was expected to pay the cost of flying the dog to the United States on a commercial flight. The cost of the flight, including a human transport attendant, fees, licenses, and other paperwork, can reach several thousand dollars. Nonprofit organizations such as Mission K9 Rescue and the American Humane Association (AHA) have helped to reunite dogs with their former handlers. In just one year, the AHA paid to bring home twenty-one MWDs retired from overseas bases at a cost of up to $6,000 each.

This process changed late in 2015 when President Obama signed the 2016 National Defense Authorization Act. The act is hundreds of pages long and is filled with provisions that regulate military spending of all kinds. In those pages are a few short paragraphs that lay out the new plan for foreign-based MWDs at retirement. The new law says that the US military must return foreign-based dogs to the United States when they retire and pay for the costs of transportation. Once back in the United States, the dogs become eligible for adoption through the usual process.

Robin Ganzert, chief executive officer and president of the AHA, said about the new regulations that "all military working dogs will be guaranteed a ride home and retirement on U.S. soil. And best of all, the people who know these dogs better than anyone—their handlers who served bravely alongside them on the hot desert sands of Iraq and Afghanistan and on bases around the world—will be given the first rights at adopting these canine heroes."

VETS FOR MWDS

Maybe you have an older dog at home. Maybe she's a little stiff in the hips or he limps when he runs. Maybe your mom has to take the dog to the veterinarian now and then. The dogs may have aches and pains, but many of them—like older people—have a lot of good years ahead of them. However, MWDs can have problems most dogs never face. Because of their years of extreme activity, many have arthritis—degeneration of the joints of their hips, elbows, or spine. Some received serious combat injuries and may have even lost an eye or a leg, perhaps from being hit by an IED. Sprained ankles, toes, and damaged footpads seem like minor injuries, but they can prevent a retired MWD from enjoying retirement. Good veterinary care and loving families can help these heroes live the best possible life.

While the US military gives MWDs the world's best veterinarian care during their working lives, medical care becomes the responsibility of the adoptive family upon retirement. The cost of caring for a retired MWD can be high. The dogs may need surgery, physical therapy, and medications. "If [the dogs] need veterinarian services, I think the government should do that," former army dog handler Jerry Witt said in a newspaper interview. "They have served, and served with honor, and they deserve to be taken care of, just like any other veteran."

Organizations large and small are banding together to help provide free or low-cost care for retired MWDs. For example, Courtney Griffin is a student at Mississippi State University's College of Veterinary Medicine. She knows Karl Stefanowicz and Dustin Weeks and their MWDs Maci and Iva. Army Captain Teri Vaughn, a veterinarian for MWDs, had recently signed off on the dogs' retirement paperwork. Vaughn thought the dogs would benefit greatly from physical therapy. "Therapy for the dogs was cost prohibitive for Karl and Dustin," Courtney says, because the therapy costs about $500 for ten sessions. But her class of future veterinarians—the Class of 2018—was looking for a project. "I couldn't think of a more noble cause, so I brought the idea to my classmates and everyone was on board!"

Courtney and her classmates started the Vets for Vets program. "The first ten sessions for each dog were paid in full from money that my class raised." Donations solicited from alumni and friends of the college paid for a second round of treatments for Maci and Iva. "Like most other retired military dogs, they both suffered from severe degenerative joint disease that comes from long days of difficult work in harsh environments, like the desert climate in Iraq and Afghanistan," Courtney says. "The hard, rocky terrain really takes a toll on their joints, resulting in pretty significant mobility issues later in life. Maci fell off a rock formation in Afghanistan, which caused further injury to his hip joints."

Courtney explains, "The two major tools we use to facilitate their rehabilitation are the water treadmill [in which a dog walks on a submerged treadmill to build muscle mass] and laser therapy [in which the vet aims laser beams at damaged tissues to stimulate healing]. The water treadmill helps the dogs regain full range of motion in their weakened limbs. The laser therapy works by increasing blood flow, decreasing inflammation, and encouraging growth of healthy tissue." Did the therapy help? "Another veterinarian evaluated Maci and Iva after their first ten sessions and was thrilled with their progress. She noted increased muscle mass, decreased pain levels, and an increased range of motion in the affected joints," Courtney said.

Karl and Dustin were also happy with the results. "Maci is like a puppy again since starting the treatment," Karl says. "I can see he is better at managing his hip issues, and he's become more social and outgoing. It's great to watch him interact with people." Dustin agrees. "This is absolutely a great program. I've never seen anything like it in my work with canines." Several organizations are trying to change the laws so that the US government will pay for ongoing medical care for retired MWDs—just like it does for retired soldiers.

CANINE PTSD

Dogs—like people—can also suffer post-traumatic stress disorder (PTSD), a mental health condition that may occur when a person or dog experiences a life-threatening, terrifying, or horrifying event, such as military combat, assault, serious injury, and other traumas. The resulting anxiety affects many aspects of life. For example, in the case of soldiers, they may become deeply depressed, suffer nightmares and terrifying flashbacks, or have trouble sleeping, getting along with others, or holding down a job. Iraq and Afghanistan Veterans of America, a nonprofit advocacy group, estimates that one out of five veterans returning from combat in those war zones is diagnosed with PTSD or depression.

About 5 to 10 percent of military working dogs used in combat zones develop post-traumatic stress disorder as well. Veterinarians and military leaders officially recognized canine PTSD in 2011 when previously deployed dogs began showing up at Lackland's Holland Military Working Dog Hospital—arguably the best veterinary facility in the world for dogs—with problems similar to those in people living with PTSD. The dogs' symptoms included anxiety, increased startle response, trying to run away, being withdrawn, shaking, hiding, and showing an inability or reluctance to perform familiar tasks such as sniffing out a bomb. Some dogs, like some people, can shrug off traumatic events, while others shut down completely.

Saying Good-Bye

Military working dogs often receive funerals with full honors befitting their status as a valuable member of the US armed forces. At some services for MWDs, buglers play the military call known as "Taps." Families of the dogs receive folded American flags in the same way they would at a soldier's funeral. At military bases, memorial services may be televised or broadcast. During Rex's funeral *(below)* in 2015 at California's Edwards Air Force Base, Andy Lansdowne, Rex's last handler, said, "He served his nation and put his life on the line protecting the ones he loved stateside and in Afghanistan." At Rex's funeral, an empty kennel near the American flag represented the life Rex gave to protect the nation's freedom. A leash symbolized the eternal bond between dog and handler, while an upside-down bucket was a reminder that Rex no longer needed food or water. After the memorial service, other handlers sang, prayed, and with their dogs paid their final respects to Rex.

Staff Sergeant James Martin, who handles MWDs, spoke of his dog Fiona at her funeral at Mississippi's Keesler Air Force Base. "We don't treat the military working dog any different than we do our service members. To us, they are service members and when they do pass on, we give them the same respect." Fiona was cremated, and her ashes returned to her family.

Breston's handler, David Yaronczyk, said of his dog at his funeral at Illinois's Scott Air Force Base, "I will always remember how great of a partner, friend, and family member he was. Breston will be truly missed and always remembered."

During a ceremony for MWD Emir in Fort Carson, Colorado, owner Lanai Singh read Emir's last will and testament. It said, "Thanks to everybody who made the last year and a half one of the most exciting and happy times of my life. Every day was joyful and I will watch over you as Angel Emir."

Veterinarians treat canine PTSD with rest, play, and antianxiety or antidepressant medications. About half of these dogs can return to their military duties. The others are assigned to less stressful jobs or are retired from the military. Sometimes, when stressed veterans and stressed dogs retire together, both can benefit from being together in a relaxed civilian setting.

Sergeant First Class Matthew Bessler developed PTSD after twenty years in the US Army. His MWD Michael has PTSD too. They help each other cope. "Michael [a Belgian Malinois] is a brother," said Sergeant Bessler. "He needs me just as much as I need him." In fact, Bessler credits Michael with preventing him from committing suicide. "[If I had killed myself], that's not being fair to the dog, not being fair to that partner who's stood beside me forever."

Gina, a highly trained bomb-sniffing dog, sits with Staff Sergeant Chris Kench at the kennel at Peterson Air Force Base in Colorado Springs, Colorado. Ordinarily playful, Gina returned from Iraq in 2009 after months of door-to-door searches and noisy explosions that left her cowering and fearful. Back in the United States, a military veterinarian diagnosed her as having PTSD.

THE FUTURE OF MILITARY WORKING DOGS

Most American combat troops left Iraq in 2011. The war in Afghanistan formally ended in 2014, and the last remaining ten thousand troops were due to leave by the end of 2017. A few hundred American advisers and Army Special Forces troops remain in both countries and in Syria as well. Fewer American soldiers in the Middle East mean fewer dogs. At least twenty-five hundred MWDs served in Iraq and Afghanistan at the height of the two wars, and many more served at US military bases at home and abroad. By late 2015, only seventeen hundred US MWDs remained in military service worldwide. Therefore, the programs to train dogs to detect IEDs have decreased in size, resulting in fewer MWDs trained for that work.

However, the Taliban has regained some of the land it lost in Afghanistan. And what was once the Iraqi branch of al-Qaeda has become the deadly Iraq- and Syria-based international terrorist organization known as ISIS (Islamic State in Iraq and Syria), often called ISIL (Islamic State of Iraq and the Levant—referring to countries of the eastern shore of the Mediterranean). For that reason, some experts believe American troops should remain in the Middle East for much longer, and US military engagement is slowly on the increase in Iraq and in Syria as Americans join other countries to fight ISIS-led terrorism in those countries.

Will MWDs be joining in the fight against ISIS? That question may have been answered in April 2016 when a group of British commandos, part of the elite Special Air Services, encountered about fifty ISIS militants armed with two Toyota-mounted machine guns near Mosul in northern Iraq. The commandos left their vehicles and scrambled for cover while taking fire from three directions. However, the commandos had a secret weapon of their own—an American dog handler and his MWD, who were attached to the group. When the handler released his German shepherd, the ISIS militants tried to shoot it but missed. The dog leaped at one of them, tearing into his face and neck, and then quickly attacked a second militant, mangling his arms and limbs. The militants screamed and fled. "The dog did its job and returned to its handler with its tail wagging," an unidentified source said. US fighter jets swooped in to bomb the terrorists. No British, American, or canine casualties were reported during this encounter.

Former Marine Corps dog handler Bret Reynolds, who worked with MWD

Bernie, believes military working dogs will always have a place. "Even if there are no dogs in war zones, there is plenty of work in military bases in the United States and abroad. For example, wherever the president goes, dog teams go with him. The Secret Service picks MWDs as opposed to police dogs for this work."

Emily Pieracci adds, "MWDs will continue to train during times of peace in order to maintain readiness. Training MWDs takes a great deal of time; it's not something you can stop and start suddenly. It takes years to get MWDs fully trained and you have to maintain a level of readiness in order to deploy MWD teams quickly if needed."

John Burnam strongly believes in the importance of military working dogs. "Based on what I learned from my experience in Vietnam, and the current use and deployment of our nation's military working dog teams, I don't see much change for the future. MWDs have proven their worth since they were first deployed on the battlefields of WW II," he says. "MWDs are proving to be more and more dependable in saving lives and in protecting American assets in the Middle East and here in the United States. This makes them irreplaceable for the foreseeable future."

THE US MILITARY WORKING DOG TEAMS NATIONAL MONUMENT

John Burnam and other former handlers worked tirelessly for several years to promote the building of a national monument to honor military working dog teams that had served the United States. The US Congress agreed to the proposal with the stipulation that it could not be built on National Park Service land and that no government money could be used for the project. So in 2008, Burnam and his associates founded a nonprofit organization called the John Burnam Monument Foundation to raise money to pay for the project. Dozens of corporate sponsors and hundreds of individuals contributed money toward the $2 million price tag.

The US military agreed to provide land for the monument at Lackland Air Force Base where most US military working dogs are trained. The monument *(below right)* represents dogs and handlers who served in all wars from World War II to those in Iraq and Afghanistan. The monument is a bronze sculpture in which a 9-foot-tall (2.7 m) handler, dressed in full combat gear, stands with a Doberman, Labrador retriever, German shepherd, and Belgian Malinois—the four breeds of dogs used most often as MWDs since World War II. The large wall behind the figures provides history and information about dog teams, while the flags represent the five branches of the US military: the army, marine corps, navy, air force, and coast guard.

John Burnam wrote in his 2014 book *Canine Warrior: How a Vietnam Scout Dog Inspired a National Monument*, "A share of the credit for our nation's freedom belongs to the war dog serving alongside his master on the battlefield. Together, they have always strived valiantly, as a team, to defend their ground, because they knew that, in the end, victory is saving American lives. . . . I have now accomplished my mission by building a national monument to honor them all forever!"

SOURCE NOTES

4 Joel Townsend, quoted in "Man's Best Friend, a Soldier's 'Battle Buddy,'" DVIDS, March 4, 2009, https://www .dvidshub.net/news/30710/mans-best-friend-soldiers-battle-buddy#. VfjJChFVhHw.

5 Mike Dowling, *Sergeant Rex: The Unbreakable Bond between a Marine and His Military Working Dog* (New York: Atria, 2011), 7.

6 Ibid., 74.

7–8 Ibid., 13.

8 Ibid., 25.

8 Ibid., 55.

8 Ibid., 27.

9 Ibid., 169.

9 Ibid., 169.

9–10 Ibid., 118.

10 Ibid., 279.

10 Ibid., 286.

10 Ibid., 288–289.

11 Megan Leavey, quoted in James O'Rourke, "Ex-Marine Hopes to Adopt the Canine Partner She Served With," *USA Today,* last modified March 11, 2012, http://usatoday30.usatoday.com/ news/nation /story/2012-03-09/marine-military-service-dog-reunite/53431138/1.

11 Megan Leavey, quoted in *CBS New York,* December 27, 2012, "Beloved Bomb-Sniffing Dog Who Retired to Live with Marine Handler Dies," http://newyork.cbslocal.com/2012/12/27/beloved-bomb -sniffing-dog-who-retired-to-live-with-marine-handler-dies/.

12 John Burnam, *A Soldier's Best Friend: Scout Dogs and Their Handlers in the Vietnam War* (New York: Union Square Press/Sterling Publishing, 2008), 171.

12 Ibid., 172.

13 Ibid., 69.

13 Ibid., 79.

13 Ibid., 83.

14 Ibid., 96.

14 "John Burnam and Clipper," YouTube video, 12:29, posted by John Burnam, March 14, 2013, https://www.youtube.com /watch?v=qyDUBpPKkzU.

15 Burnam, *Soldier's Best Friend,* 144.

15 Ibid., 141-142.

16–17 Ibid., 244.

17   Ibid., 244–245.

17   John Burnam, interviews with author, August 26 to September 20, 2015.

18   Burnam, *Soldier's Best Friend*, 273.

18   Marcus Terentius Varro, quoted in "History and Origin of the Molosser Breeds," Bulldog Information Library, accessed May 7, 2016, http://www.bulldoginformation.com/molossers-mastiff-breeds-history.html.

22   Ralph Popp, quoted in Jeremy P. Amick, "The Dogs of War WWII Veteran Helped Train War Dogs as Part of Army's K-9 Corps," *California Democrat*, December 30, 2015, http://www.californiademocrat.com /news/2015/dec/30/dogs-war-wwii-veteran-helped-train-war-dogs-part-a/.

23   John J. Pershing, quoted in Gillian Kane, "Sergeant Stubby," *Slate*, May 7, 2014, . http://www.slate.com /articles/news_and_politics/history/2014/05/dogs_of_war_sergeant_stubby_the_u_s_army_s_original_and_still_most_highly.html.

24–25 Kate Kelly, "The Government Asked for Pets for Defense in the 1940s," *Huffington Post*, last modified October 3, 2011, http://www.huffingtonpost.com/kate-kelly/dogs-world-war-2_b_916760.html.

25   Ibid.

27   Mrs. Edward Jo Conally, quoted in "Dogs and National Defense: WWII & Korea War Dog History II," US War Dogs Association, accessed May 7, 2016, http://www.uswardogs.org/id25.html.

28   Lisa Rogak, *The Dogs of War: The Courage, Love, and Loyalty of Military Working Dogs* (New York: Thomas Dunne, 2011), 60.

28   "Dogs and National Defense," US War Dogs Association.

28   Burnam, *Soldier's Best Friend*, 119-120.

29   Ibid., 114.

29   "John Burnam and Clipper," YouTube video.

30   Burnam, *Soldier's Best Friend*, 147.

30   Ron Aiello, quoted in Gina Joseph, "War Dogs: Serendipity Reunites Two Marines," *Macomb (MI) Daily*, last modified September 27, 2015, http://www.macombdaily.com/veterans/20150925/war-dogs-serendipity -reunites-two-marines#author1.

32   Ron Aiello, quoted in Lisa Hoffman, "Seeking to Honor America's Four-Footed Soldiers," Vietnam Dog Handler Association, May 27, 2002, http://www.vdha.us/content230.html.

32   Carl Dobbins, quoted in Lisa Rogak, *Dogs of War*, 60.

32   Spencer Dixon, quoted in "War Dogs of Vietnam," YouTube video, 11:27, posted by "ragman240AHC," January 6, 2015, https://www.youtube.com/watch?v=ewwu4nVGu-8.

32   Burnam, *Soldier's Best Friend*, 279.

32   Charlie Cargo, quoted in "War Dogs of Vietnam," YouTube video.

33 Beverly Gainer, quoted in "War Dog Given Hero's Funeral," Hartsdale Pet Cemetery and Crematory, February 21, 2001,. https://www.hartsdalepetcrematory.com/news/war-dog-given-heros-funeral/.

34 Stewart Hilliard, quoted in Randy Roughton, "Quality Breeding: DOD Program Strives to Establish Proven Bloodlines for Military Working Dogs," *Airman,* January 20, 2015, http://airman.dodlive .mil/2015/01/quality-breeding/.

36 Ibid.

37 Ibid.

37 DoD Military Working Dog Breedem Program's Facebook page, accessed July 18, 2016.

37–38 Bernadine Green, quoted in Elaine Sanchez, "Breeding Programs Turns Puppies into Troops," American Forces Press Service, February 7, 2012, http://archive.defense.gov/news/newsarticle.aspx?id=67089.

38 Lora Harrist, interview with author, November 30, 2015.

38 Ibid.

39 Ibid.

39 Ibid.

40 Stewart Hilliard, interview with author, November 23, 2015.

40 Ibid.

43 Lillian Hardy, quoted in Rogak, *Dogs of War,* 103.

43 Sharif DeLarge, quoted in Roughton, "Quality Breeding."

44 Rogak, *Dogs of War,* 11.

45 Paul Baldwin, quoted in Mitch Shaw, "An Elite Group of Four-Footed Airmen Training at Hill," *Navy Times,* July 10, 2015, http://www.navytimes.com/story/military/2015/07/10/an-elite-group-of-four -legged-airmen-training-at-hill/29951185/.

46 Ben Standley, quoted in Chuck Wullenjohn, "Camels, Other Livestock Help Train Military Dogs at YPG," *Yuma Sun,* November 1, 2015. http://www.yumasun.com/business/camels-other-livestock-help-train -military-dogs-at-ypg/article_6c29d614-7f5f-11e5-8261-c7f97092c23e.html.

47 Suzette Clemans, quoted in Caitlin Bevel, "Marine Dog Teams Sniff out Trouble," military.com, October 28, 2015, http://www.military.com/daily-news/2015/10/28/marine-dog-teams-sniff-out -trouble.html.

47 Gerry Proctor, quoted in Rogak, *Dogs of War,* 81.

47 Anonymous Austrian special forces soldier, quoted in Rogak, *Dogs of War,* 82.

48 William Egelston, quoted in Miranda Faughn, "Provost and Paws," DVIDS, October 15, 2015, https://www.dvidshub.net/news/180040/provost-and-paws#.VjFC236rRMw.

48–49 Teri Messina, quoted in Rogak, *Dogs of War,* 116.

49 Maria Goodavage, *Soldier Dogs: The Untold Story of America's Canine Heroes* (New York: Dutton, 2012), 95.

49 Ibid.

49 James Walker, quoted in Peter Tyson, "Dogs' Dazzling Sense of Smell," *PBS NOVA*, October 4, 2012, http://www .pbs.org/wgbh/nova/nature/dogs-sense-of-smell.html.

52 Angela Lowe, personal interview with author, September 28, 2015.

52 Ibid.

53 Ibid.

53 Ibid.

54 Mike Dowling, "The 9 Biggest Myths about Military Working Dogs," *We Are the Mighty*, February 4, 2015, http://www.wearethemighty.com/lists/military-working-dogs-myths.

55 Anthony Andrews, quoted in Vanessa Villarreal, "Military Working Dog Handlers: It's the Best Job Ever," US Army, July 8, 2015 https://www.army.mil/article/151877 /Military_working_dog_ handlers__It_s_the_best_job_ever_/.

55 Dowling, *Sergeant Rex*, 41.

58 Kent Ferrell, quoted in *Glory Hounds*, YouTube video, 1:24:05, posted by "k9kazooie," January 13, 2014, https://www.youtube.com/watch?v=iM5oSvXAUBI.

58 Justin Kitts, quoted in "Valuable Noses," *Airman*, November 1, 2011, http://airman.dodlive .mil/ tag/staff-sgt-justin-kitts/.

58 Brandon Liebert, quoted in Goodavage, *Soldier Dogs*, 33.

59 Mark Vierig, quoted in Goodavage, *Soldier Dogs*, 209.

60 Burnam, interviews.

60 Karl Stefanowicz, interviews with author, September 2015.

62 Barack Obama, quoted in Nicholas Schmidle, "Getting Bin Laden," *New Yorker*, August 8, 2011, http://www .newyorker.com/magazine/2011/08/08/getting-bin-laden.

62 Unidentified SEAL commander called "James," quoted in Schmidle, "Getting Bin Laden."

63 Allison Brekke, quoted in Dillian Bamman, "Vet Clinic Supports MWD Program with Care, Training," US Air Force, July 22, 2015, http://www.af.mil/News/ArticleDisplay/tabid/223/ Article/610543 /vet-clinic-supports-mwd-program-with-care-training.aspx.

64 Emily Pieracci, interview with author, September 17, 2015.

65 Ibid.

65 Ibid.

65 Ibid.

65–66 Ibid.

66 Lowe, interview with author, September 28, 2015.

66 Stefanowicz, interviews.

67 Lance Brennan, quoted in Jeff Mullin, "2 Vance Dog Teams Helped Protect Pope Francis during Visit," *Enidnews.com,* October 15, 2015, http://www.enidnews.com/news/vas_inside_the_gate/vance-dog-teams-helped -protect-pope-francis-during-visit/article_19202e82-9449-52d9-a85b-82841fc8ee8c.html.

68 "Mission," Dogs on Deployment, accessed May 7, 2016, http://www.dogsondeployment.org/page/mission.

68 Dogs on Deployment's Facebook page, photos, Argos, November 1 and 9, 2015, https://www.facebook.com/DogsonDeployment/photos/pb.152297704839495.-2207520000.1461885366./875289909206934/?type=3&theater.

68 Ibid.

70 Greg Madrid, quoted in Shannon Wiggins, "MCLB Canine Wins Prestigious Award," *WALB News,* October 8, 2015, http://www.walb.com/story/30221870/mclb-canine-wins-prestigious-award.

70 Jan McLoughlin, quoted in Erika I. Ritchie, "Camp Pendleton War Dog Loses Leg in Bomb Blast, Gets Highest Military Honor," *Orange County (CA) Register,* last modified April 29, 2016, http://www.ocregister.com/articles/lucca -713832-willingham-dog.html.

71 Bret Reynolds, interview with author, September 24, 2015.

71 Bill Childress, quoted in Rebecca Frankel, "WDotW: Actually, No, There Are No Military Dogs Left Behind," *Foreign Policy,* September 19, 2014, http://foreignpolicy.com/2014/09/19/wdotw-actually-no -there-are-no-military-dogs-left-behind/.

72 "MWD Adoptions FAQ's," United States War Dogs Association, accessed May 7, 2016, http://www.uswardogs.org/mwd-adoptions-faqs/.

73 Hilliard, interview.

73–74 Reynolds, interview.

75 Stefanowicz, interviews.

76 Ibid.

76 Charles Hardesty, interview with author, October 15, 2015.

77 Ibid.

77 Rebecca Frankel, *War Dogs: Tales of Canine Heroism, History, and Love* (New York: Palgrave Macmillan, 2014), 133.

77 Hardesty, interview.

77 Dustin Weeks, interview with author, November 18, 2015.

77 Ibid.

78 Ibid.

78 Ibid.

78 Ibid.

78 Ibid.

79 Mission K9 Rescue Facebook page, accessed May 7, 2016, https://www.facebook.com / MissionK9/posts/1090217924329413.

79 Ibid.

80 Ibid.

80 Ibid.

81 Thomas E. Ricks and Rebecca Frankel, "Rebecca's War Dog of the Year," *Foreign Policy,* May 6, 2016, http://foreignpolicy.com/2016/05/06/rebeccas-war-dog-of-the -year-im-off-to-phoenix-next-week-to-adopt-dyngo/.

81 Nofo Lilo, quoted in Ricks and Frankel, "Rebecca's War Dog."

81 Ricks and Frankel, "Rebecca's War Dog."

82 Robin Ganzert, quoted in "Finally, Victory for America's Military Dogs!" *American Humane Association Blog,* November 20, 2015, http://americanhumaneblog.org/finally-victory-for-americas-military-dogs/.

83 Jerry Witt, quoted in Meg Jones, "U.S. War Dogs Serve with Honor but Don't Get Retiree Health Care," *Milwaukee Journal Sentinel,* July 25, 2015, http://www.jsonline.com/news/wisconsin/us-war-dogs-serve-with-honor-but-dont-get-retiree-health-care-b99539428z1-318552841.html.

83 Courtney Griffin, interview with author, November 20, 2015.

84 Ibid.

84 Karl Stefanowicz, quoted in Karen Templeton, "Mississippi State Vet Students Help Military Dogs," Mississippi State University, August 12, 2015, http://www.msstate.edu/newsroom / article/2015/08/mississippi-state-vet-students-help-military-dogs/.

84 Dustin Weeks in Templeton, "Mississippi State Vet Students."

85 Andy Lansdowne, quoted in Rebecca Amber, "Team Edwards Says Goodbye to Airman's Best Friend," Edwards Air Force Base, August 25, 2015, http://www.edwards.af.mil/news/story. asp?id=123455201.

85 James Martin, quoted in Doug Walker, "Fiona Given a Hero's Final Send-off at Keesler," *WLOX,* July 22, 2015, http://www.wlox.com/story /29608700/fiona-given-a-heros-final-send-off-at-keesler.

85 David Yaronczyk, quoted in Kiana Brothers, "Military Working Dog Laid to Rest," July 9, 2015, https://www .dvidshub.net/news/170864/military-working-dog-laid-rest#.VnyOk_krJMw.

85 Lanai Singh, quoted in Andrea Stone, "Memorial Ceremony Honors Service of Military Working Dog," US Army, June 27, 2013, http://www.army.mil/article/106517/Memorial_ceremony_ honors_service_of_military_working_dog/.

86 Matthew Bessler, quoted in Sarah Kershaw, "A Soldier and His Combat Dog Both Returned from Iraq with PTSD—and Found Support in Each Other," *Washington Post,* July 2, 2015,

http://www.washingtonpost.com/news/inspired-life/wp/2015/07/02/a-decorated-soldier-and-his -beloved-combat-dog-both-returned-from-iraq-with-ptsd-and-found-support-in-each-other/.

87 Anonymous, quoted in Adam Linehan, "ISIS Fighters Reportedly Savaged by American Military Working Dog," *Task and Purpose,* May 9, 2016, http://taskandpurpose.com/isis-fighters-reportedly -savaged-american-military-working-dog/.

88 Reynolds, interview.

88 Pierraci, interviews.

88 Burnam, interviews.

89 John Burnam, *Canine Warrior: How a Vietnam Scout Dog Inspired a National Monument* (Fort Bragg: Lost Coast, 2014), 352.

GLOSSARY

canine post-traumatic stress disorder (PTSD): a mental health condition that can affect dogs after a life-threatening, terrifying, or horrific event, such as military combat, assault, and other trauma. Dogs with PTSD are anxious, fearful, and withdrawn. About half the dogs with PTSD are unable to continue their military duties, while the other half recover with rest, play, and medication.

deployment: sending troops, dogs, and other military personnel to serve at bases or in conflicts overseas or away from their home bases

handler: the man or woman who trains and works with a military working dog over a period of time

improvised explosive device (IED): a device made from easily available materials and explosives for the purpose of injuring or killing others. IEDs are usually hidden in abandoned buildings, cars, and homes or under sandy roads and ditches. Triggered remotely or when a person or a dog unexpectedly comes in contact with the IED trip wire, the devices cause tremendous damage, injury, and even death.

insurgent: a person who revolts against civil authority or an established government. The term can also refer to people independently fighting US forces and their allies in Iraq, Afghanistan, and Syria.

Islamic State in Iraq and Syria (ISIS): also called the Islamic State of Iraq and the Levant (ISIL), this international terrorist organization is committed to destroying the modern Islamic State to restore the Islamic caliphate, a form of Islamic government in which a person considered to be the political and religious successor to Muhammad (who founded Islam in the seventh century CE), rules all the Muslim world.

kennel master: the soldier in charge of military working dogs and their handlers at a military base

military working dog (MWD): a specially trained dog owned by the US Department of Defense that works with a handler to perform duties such as bomb and drug detection and to chase, catch, and detain intruders and suspects. The dogs also patrol bases and military camps and provide protection for high-profile political leaders and other public figures. After retiring from the military, the dogs are sometimes reassigned to police departments or to security agencies.

Not Forgotten Fountain: part of the US Military Working Dog Teams National Monument, this fountain was dedicated in 2013 to commemorate the military working dogs left behind after the Vietnam War. The fountain also provides drinking water for visiting dogs and handlers.

al-Qaeda: a global militant Islamist organization founded by Osama bin Laden in 1988. The group was responsible for the September 11, 2001, terrorist attacks in New York City and in Arlington, Virginia.

Robby's Law: the US Congress passed this law in 2000 to promote the adoption of military working dogs by former handlers instead of the disposal of the dogs by other methods, including euthanasia (except when medically necessary).

Taliban: an Islamic fundamentalist political movement based primarily in Afghanistan. The group ruled that nation from 1996 until 2001. It promotes a strict interpretation of Sharia, or Islamic law.

temporary duty (TDY) assignment: a short deployment to a war zone or to a military base

US Military Working Dog Teams National Monument: a monument at Lackland Air Force Base in San Antonio, Texas. Dedicated in 2013, the bronze sculptures of the monument include a handler and four military working dogs, as representatives of the handler-dog teams that have served the US military since World War II. The monument honors dog teams in all branches of the US military.

SELECTED BIBLIOGRAPHY

Burnam, John C. *Canine Warrior: How a Vietnam Scout Dog Inspired a National Monument.* Fort Bragg, CA: Lost Coast, 2014.

Dowling, Mike. "9 Biggest Myths about Military Working Dogs." *We Are the Mighty,* February 4, 2015. http://www.wearethemighty.com/lists/military-working-dogs-myths.

———. *Sergeant Rex: The Unbreakable Bond between a Marine and His Military Working Dog.* New York: Atria, 2011.

Frankel, Rebecca. "WDotW: Actually, No, There Are No Military Dogs Left Behind." *Foreign Policy,* September 19, 2014. http://foreignpolicy.com/2014/09/19/wdotw-actually-no-there-are-no-military-dogs-left-behind/.

———. "The Forgotten Heroes of America's Past Wars: Military Working Dogs." *Task and Purpose,* October 14, 2015. http://taskandpurpose.com/the-forgotten-heroes-of-americas-past-wars-military-working-dogs/.

———. *War Dogs: Tales of Canine Heroism, History, and Love.* New York: Palgrave Macmillan, 2014.

Kelly, Kate. "The Government Asked for Pets for Defense in the 1940s." *Huffington Post,* last modified October 3, 2011. http://www.huffingtonpost.com/kate-kelly/dogs-world-war-2_b_916760.html.

Rogak, Lisa. *The Dogs of War: The Courage, Love, and Loyalty of Military Working Dogs.* New York: Thomas Dunne, 2011.

Templeton, Karen. "Mississippi State Vet Students Help Military Dogs." *Mississippi State University,* August 12, 2015. http://www.msstate.edu/newsroom/article/2015/08/mississippi-state-vet-students-help-military-dogs/.

Tyson, Peter. "Dogs' Dazzling Sense of Smell." *PBS NOVA,* October 4, 2012. http://www.pbs.org/wgbh/nova/nature/dogs-sense-of-smell.html.

FURTHER INFORMATION

Books

Burnam, John C. *A Soldier's Best Friend: Scout Dogs and Their Handlers in the Vietnam War.* New York: Union Square, 2008. The author tells the story of his tour of duty in the Vietnam War and the three MWDs with which he worked there.

Goodavage, Maria. *Soldier Dogs: The Untold Story of America's Canine Heroes.* New York: Dutton, 2012. Based on many personal interviews and visits to American bases, this book discusses what military working dogs do, their training, and the bond between dog and handler.

Kadohata, Cynthia. *Cracker! The Best Dog in Vietnam.* New York: Atheneum Books for Young Readers, 2007. Newbery-winning novelist Kadohata tells the story of military working dog Cracker and his young handler in the Vietnam War. Told in alternating points of view between the dog and handler, the story is ideal for ages ten and up.

Patent, Dorothy Hinshaw. *Dogs on Duty.* New York: Bloomsbury, 2014. Readers of all ages will enjoy this thorough and colorful exploration of the modern military war dog and how it is selected, trained, and deployed.

Videos

Barrell, Ryan. "Conan O'Brien Trains with a Military Dog Unit at Al Udeid Air Base in Qatar." *Huffington Post,* January 27, 2016. http://www.huffingtonpost.co.uk/2016/01/27/conan-o-brien-trains-military-dog-unit-al-udeid-air-base-qatar_n_9087094.html. This article includes a 6.17-minute humorous video of Conan O'Brien "training" with a MWD at the US Air Force base in Qatar. He jokes with the handlers, then dresses in protective gear as a dog chases him and brings him down.

"Dogs of War." Military.com video, 3:18, April 10, 2015. http://www.military.com/video/operations-and-strategy/military-tactics/dogs-of-war/4165410101001/. Military war dogs have saved tens of thousands of lives since the beginning of their military service. This short video describes their contributions to American war efforts since World War II.

"Dogs in WW II: The Use of War Dogs, 1943 War Department (US Army); K-9 Corps." YouTube video, 11:55. Posted by "Jeff Quitney," September 17, 2013. https://www.youtube.com/watch?v=NTb2ZEAm7Ms. This video shows how the US military used dogs in WW II for various duties, such as messenger dogs carrying supplies as well as messages.

Glory Hounds. YouTube video, 1:24:05. Posted by "k9kazooie," January 13, 2014. https://www.youtube.com/watch?v=iM5oSvXAUBI. Filmed in Afghanistan, this video profiles four military dogs and their handlers in the war zone as they locate insurgents and dangerous explosives.

"Hero War Dog Skydives with Soldier." *National Geographic* video, 3:44, June 12, 2014. http://news.nationalgeographic.com/news/2014/06/140612-war-dog-parachute-pets-skydive-jump-george-hw-bush/. See MWD Layka make her first tandem parachute jump from a small plane using a newly designed parachute harness.

Neaves, Alicia. "Military Dogs Trained in San Antonio Go on to Serve around the World." KENS5 video,

3:23, May 3, 2016. http://www.kens5.com/news/local/a-look-inside-jbsa-lacklands-military-working-dog-breeding-program/165397021. Watch puppy training at Lackland Air Force Base, where personnel train American MWDs.

Rebecca Frankel Interview Part 1 02/09/15." Teamcoco, Conan, February 10, 2015. http://teamcoco.com/video/rebecca-frankel-pt-1-02-09-15. Conan O'Brien interviews MWD handler Charles Hardesty and his dog Robbie, along with author Rebecca Frankel *(War Dogs: Tales of Canine Heroism, History, and Love).* The 4.35-minute excerpt shows Hardesty and Frankel talking about MWDs, and Robbie plays with a Kong.

The True Story of the Vietnam War—War Dogs—America's Forgotten Heroes. YouTube video, 1:20:10. Posted by "Gidi Ben Dor," January 3, 2014. https://www.youtube.com/watch?v=gyH1T9Y7u8w. This documentary showcases the dogs that worked to help their human handlers in combat during the Vietnam War.

War Dogs of the Pacific. Harris Done, 2008. This forty-six-minute documentary tells the incredible true story of the marine war dog platoons of World War II and the unique bond that formed between the marines and their dogs. Their success at finding the hidden enemy saved countless lives in the Pacific.

Websites

Department of Defense MWD Breeding Program

https://www.facebook.com/DoDMWDBreedingProgram

The Department of Defense page describes in detail the military working dog breeding and training program at Lackland Air Force Base.

Dogs on Deployment

https://www.facebook.com/DogsonDeployment/

This organization helps find temporary homes for members of the military and veterans who may be deployed or otherwise unable to care for their animals.

K9s for Warriors

https://www.facebook.com/K9sforWarriors

This organization provides and trains service dogs for American soldiers and military personnel suffering from post-traumatic stress disorder.

K9 Soldiers, Inc.

1 Bush Farm Lane

Frenchtown, NJ 08825-3701

908-996-1234

http://www.k9soldiers.org/home.html

This nonprofit organization works to support deployed K9 teams worldwide, including sending difficult-to-find dog-related supplies to bases overseas. It also works with the Argos Project, designed to provide injured soldiers with trained therapy and companion dogs when they return from deployment.

Military Working Dogs

https://www.facebook.com/MilitaryWorkingDogs/?fref=ts
This organization supports military working dogs and their handlers. Click on the link for videos, photos, additional links, and discussions about military working dogs.

Mission K9 Rescue

3529 Old Conejo Rd, Ste. 111
Newbury Park, CA 91320
713-589-9362
http://missionk9rescue.org/contact-mission-k9-rescue/
Mission K9 Rescue is dedicated to the service of retiring and retired military working dogs and contract working dogs. It provides assistance and support for working dogs worldwide. It rescues, reunites, and rehabilitates any retired working dog that has served people in any capacity, military or otherwise.

Operation We Are Here: Military Working Dog Resources

http://www.operationwearehere.com/MilitaryWorkingDogs.html
The group provides resources and supports for members of the US military, their families, and their working dogs. The military working dog page offers an extensive list of topics such as adopting dogs and deployment support, as well as information about books, movies, and video clips about military working dogs.

Retired Military Working Dogs

https://www.facebook.com/Retired-Military-Working-Dogs-162014883861620/
This organization celebrates and honors retired military working dogs with articles, news, photos, and updates.

United States War Dogs Association

1313 Mt. Holly Road
Burlington, NJ 08016
609-747-9340
http://www.uswardogs.org/
This is a nonprofit organization of former and current handlers of US military working dogs. Its goals include educating the public about the value of the dogs and raising funds to establish memorials. The association also helps with adopting retiring military working dogs and police canines.

Vietnam Dog Handler Association

http://www.vdha.us/
Beginning in 1993 with six Vietnam War dog handlers, this group has grown to about three thousand members. The organization educates the public so that war dogs of Vietnam and of all conflicts will not be forgotten. Members promote the group's causes in print and on film. One goal is to convince the US Postal Service to issue a war dog stamp to honor the service and sacrifice of all war dogs.

INDEX

PHOTO ACKNOWLEDGMENTS

The images in this book are used with the permission of: © iStockphoto.com/MariaArefyeva (grunge background); © iStockphoto.com/Leontura (paw print); © iStockphoto.com/Casper1774Studio (camouflage background); Sgt. Alfred V. Lopez/U.S. Marines, pp. 1, 56; U.S. Air Force photo/Staff Sgt. Perry Aston, p. 5; © ZUMA Press, Inc./Alamy, p. 6; AP Photo/Seth Wenig, p. 11; Courtesy of John Burnam , p. 12; © JBMF/Wikimedia Commons (CC BY-SA 4.0), p. 16; © Universal History Archive/UIG/Getty Images, p. 19; © Bettmann/Getty Images, pp. 21, 24, © 611 collection/Alamy, p. 22; National Archives (532371), p. 25; © Everett Collection Inc/Alamy, p. 27; © R. A. Elder/Hulton Archiveency/Getty Images, p. 29; U.S. Air Force photo/Security Forces Museum, p. 31; © Matthew Mahon/Redux, p. 36; © Lora Harrist, p. 38; © Anne McQuary/The State/MCT/Getty Images, p. 41; © Massoud HOSSAINI/Getty Images, p. 42; U.S. Air Force photo/Staff Sgt. Stacy L. Pearsal, p. 45; © Corbis RM Stills/Getty Images, p. 50; © Jupiterimages/Thinkstock, p. 51; © Laura Westlund//Independent Picture Service, p. 51 (illustrated diagram elements); U.S. Air Force photo/Senior Airman Dennis Sloan, p. 53; U.S. Army Sgt. Jason Brace/86th Infantry Brigade Combat Team/Task Force Wolverine Public Affairs, p. 61; U.S. Department of Defense, p. 62; AP Photo/Anja Niedringhaus, p. 64; © Bret Reynolds, p. 67; AP Photo/Press Association, p. 69; © Yana Paskova/Getty Images, p. 72; © Dustin Weeks, p. 78; REUTERS/Shamil Zhumatov/Newscom, p. 79; U.S. Air Force photo, p. 85; AP Photo/Ed Andrieski, p. 86; EJ Hersom/Department of Defense, p. 89.

Front cover: U.S. Air Force photo/ Staff Sgt. Stephenie Wade; © iStockphoto.com/MariaArefyeva (grunge background).

Back cover: © iStockphoto.com/MariaArefyeva (grunge background); © iStockphoto.com/Leontura (paw print).

ABOUT THE AUTHOR

Connie Goldsmith has written eighteen nonfiction books, mostly on health topics, for middle-school and young adult readers and has published more than two hundred magazine articles for adults and youth. Her latest YA book, *The Ebola Epidemic: The Fight, The Future*, was a Junior Library Guild selection. *Bombs over Bikini* was also a Junior Library Guild Selection, a Children's Book Committee at Bank Street College Best Children's Book of the Year, an Association of Children's Librarians of Northern California Distinguished Book, and an SCBWI Crystal Kite winner. She is an active member of the Society of Children's Book Writers and Illustrators and is a member of the Authors Guild. Goldsmith is also a registered nurse with a bachelor of science degree in nursing and a master of public administration degree in health care. She lives and writes near Sacramento, California.